WORKPLACE

CLUES FOR THE CLUELESS

CHRISTOPHER D. HUDSON

KATIE E. GIESER

TIMOTHY BAKER

ANN MARIE CLARK

CHRISTINE COLLIER ERICKSON

CAROL SMITH

LINDA WASHINGTON

LEN WOODS

PROMISE
PRESS
An Imprint of Barbour Publishing

Check out Barbour's exciting web sites at: www.barbourbooks.com and www.cluesfortheclueless.com

Developed and produced by the Livingstone Corporation.

Interior Design by Design Corps, Batavia, IL.

Cover Design by Robyn Martins.

Cover and Interior Artwork by Elwood Smith.

ISBN: 1-57748-740-0

Published by: Promise Press, an imprint of Barbour Publishing, Inc., P.O. Box 719 Uhrichsville, OH 44683.

TABLE OF CONTENTS

SECTION 1
FIRST THINGS FIRST 1

A High Priority..... 2
Meaningful Labor...... 8

SECTION 2
BEING A GOOD EMPLOYEE 11

Relating to the Boss..... 12
Relating to Coworkers..... 16
Intra-office Dating..... 22
The Damage of Gossip..... 29
Other Great Books to Read (Besides This One)..... 33

SECTION 3
RULES OF THE ROAD 35

Presenting Reports..... 36
E-mail Codes of Conduct..... 41
Cubicle Culture..... 44
Annoying Habits to Avoid..... 49
Preparing for Your Review..... 54

SECTION 4
BEING A GOOD BOSS 59

Getting in Touch..... 60
Good Bossing..... 64
When You Want to Say You Care..... 66
Conducting Performance Reviews..... 68
The Raise Factor..... 72
Issues of Leadership..... 76

SECTION 5
CHRISTIAN WITNESS 81

Has This Ever Happened to You?..... 82
Good Tasting Food..... 86
Blowing It Big Time..... 91

SECTION 6
CLIMBING THE CORPORATE LADDER 95

Strap on Your Hiking Boots and Climb. . .Toward a Promotion!..... 96

Passing the Buck: Responsibility..... 104

The Heat Is On. . .Performance Reviews..... 107

Image Isn't Just a Sprite Commercial..... 112

SECTION 7
WHEN IT JUST AIN'T COMIN' UP ALL ROSES 115

Take Two and Call Me in the Morning..... 116

Handling Adversity..... 120

Confrontation..... 123

Discrimination..... 127

When Your Best Isn't Good Enough..... 129

When You've Just Blown Your Deadline..... 132

SECTION 8
ETHICS 135

What's Black and White and Gray All Over? Corporate America..... 136

Everybody's Doing It. . .Stealing?! 138

Something Doesn't Look Right Here..... 140

Nip and Tuck: Expense Allocation..... 142

Integrity..... 144

Conscience: Rules, Regulations, and You..... 146

Temptation..... 148

SECTION 9
FINANCIAL 151

Contentment..... 152
Tithing..... 156
Saving..... 159
Retirement..... 161
Bringing Home the Bacon..... 164
Appropriate Benefits..... 166

SECTION 10
OFFICE ODDITIES 169

Fun Lunch Breaks..... 170
Breaking the Code: From Three-Piece Suits to Casual Friday..... 173
The Company Picnic..... 179
The Commute..... 183

SECTION 11
GETTING YOUR ACT TOGETHER 189

Fitting in Exercise..... 190

Making Budgets..... 192

Arranging Your Schedule..... 195

Decision-making..... 199

What Does It Take?..... 202

Life Outside of Work..... 205

Maintaining Friendships..... 209

Finding a Mentor..... 214

SECTION 12
FAMILY 219

Waking Up to the Grind..... 220

The Great Divorce...... 222

Making the Separation..... 226

Making the Right Moves..... 231

Kids at Work...... 235

Best Friends and Workmates..... 238

INTRODUCTION

Isn't it about time you got a raise? You *have* been faithfully serving the company for years, after all. . . .

The company will never notice a couple more long-distance calls on the next telephone bill. . . .

You *know* it's Junior's last soccer game, but the boss has to have this project completed. . . .

Sound familiar? Although it's helping put food on the table and braces on little Sally, your job can be any number of things—draining, confusing, fulfilling, challenging, addicting. . .to name a few. Issues arise that are contrary to what you know to be true. You are hounded by the feeling that you'll never have "enough." You know your family deserves better, but you just don't have time. These concerns and more, from presentations to casual Fridays, are dealt with in this book.

The recovering workaholics here at *Clues for the Clueless* have put together a little manual for you to help you anticipate or alleviate some of the stresses and issues that arise from life on the job. We're not promising to solve all your workplace woes, but we are promising a healthier, more balanced way to bring home the bacon. Sizzling inside these covers are. . .

CATCH A CLUE

A Truckload of Clues. You'll learn tips from folks who've been there, done that, and would love to help you along as well.

WIDE ANGLE

Perspective. We easily get caught up in the everyday routine of getting up for work and then falling back into bed at night. To have a more joyful attitude about what you're doing, it's helpful to take a look at the big picture. We'll help you take a step back.

WOW!

Amazing Stories and Facts. Since much of the population is involved in some sort of work, there are some fascinating stories and interesting facts. We've collected a few for you to enjoy.

DON'T FORGET

Important Reminders. Certain things are important to remember through the years. We've highlighted those for you.

THE BOTTOM LINE

The Bottom Line. We'll help you get beyond confusion by letting you know the most important stuff to
remember.

THE BIBLE SAYS

Help from Above. We've highlighted a few key
verses that will help you understand what the Bible
has to say about your work.

Whether you work in a large corporation or a small start-up, there's one
thing that's certain—you're working! You're also interacting with people,
planning, and budgeting. Before you think one more disheartening thing
about your job: *Read this book.* Feel free to read it your way: from cover to
cover or skipping around to the parts that interest you most. No matter how
you read it, you'll find it's jammed with good advice, great ideas, and
entertaining thoughts. So turn the page and start reading. . . . You'll be glad
you did!

SECTION 1

···

FIRST THINGS FIRST

A HIGH PRIORITY

Ebenezer Scrooge, one of the most well-known characters in literature, lived an imbalanced life. If you know the story of *A Christmas Carol* (who doesn't?), you know that Ebenezer, after being haunted by three ghosts, realized that he had given the highest priority to the acquisition of gold, rather than family or spiritual health. The woman who loved him sadly told him that his avarice left no place for her in his life. At the end of the story he realized that a family and "good will to all men" were more important than the "golden idol" that he had worshiped. Alas, many of us can well relate.

Quality of Time

"The balance between work, family, and church involvement is not the balance of time, but the balance of quality of time. If the quality is high, whether you're talking about one minute or one day, that makes a difference."
—Stan, who balances family, a position as church trustee, and a career at McDonald's Corporation, Oak Brook, Illinois

Three major areas of a Christian's life are family, work, and church involvement. How can a busy person juggle all of his or her responsibilities and still feel like he or she has given quality time in each area? Can a person really "have it all," or is that just a myth? Is it possible to avoid neglecting one priority in favor of another?

The American Heritage Dictionary defines *priority* as "precedence, esp. established by order of importance or urgency; an established right or precedence."

We can all agree that family, work, and church are three priorities that cannot be neglected. So, break out the juggling balls and. . .

SEEK THE LORD'S HELP

This may sound like a broken record, but it is nonetheless true. God, Who is the Source of all wisdom (see Proverbs 1:7, 4:5; James 1:5), can certainly help anyone who sincerely seeks to put first things first. As the Creator of the family, the first "Employer" (see Genesis 2:15), and the Head of the Church, He knows all of the facets of the human life.

KEEP TRACK OF IMPORTANT APPOINTMENTS

These include little Billy's violin recital, Ramona's soccer match, your trustee meeting at church, and your performance review at work. If you're prone to forgetfulness as many of us are, getting into the habit of jotting things down is a good one for a time juggler to cultivate. An electronic organizer, an IBM Palm Pilot, Franklin Planner, Daytimer—any type of scheduler—can help you keep track of where you need to be and when. Some electronic organizers even cue you in on important dates like birthdays, anniversaries, or Sweetest Day to remind you to run to Walgreen's and buy that gift.

Many busy families keep a wall calendar where important family appointments are recorded. What is your family's way of keeping track of the events in your lives?

STAY COMMITTED TO WHAT YOU VALUE MOST

As everyone knows, you make time for what you value most. Only *you* know the priorities that are of the utmost importance. Let nothing short of an emergency come between you and keeping those commitments. Many of these priorities will more than likely center around those that are key to your family (for example, your aunt Phyllis's wedding, your son's bar mitzvah).

Many busy people find the need to schedule a set time each week for family time, including dates with spouses. As Stephen Covey wrote in *The 7 Habits of Highly Effective Families*, "The most important thing is to make the commitment to do it: 'Once a week, no matter what, we will have family time together.' "

A Golden Nugget

DON'T FORGET

"Quality time is like a golden nugget in a muddy stream. Within a pan full of mud, we may find a single nugget. After much time, effort, and determination, are we then enriched with precious moments with others."
—J. Isamu Yamamoto, Christian, book author/editor, family man.

KNOW YOUR AREAS OF WEAKNESS. . .

Problems like workaholism, difficulty with confrontation, overcommitment, and such can cause an imbalance in our lives. That's why we need to honestly evaluate our weaknesses. As God said, "My grace is sufficient for you, for my power is made perfect in weakness" (2 Corinthians 12:9). That's why Paul could add, "I delight in weaknesses. . . . For when I am weak, then I am strong" (v. 10). He knew that weakness forced him to rely on God's strength.

An honest evaluation of our weaknesses includes getting to the source of what drives us. Fear? Anger? A desire for power? It also takes us to the end of ourselves.

. . .AND GIVE THOSE AREAS TO GOD

Once we've honestly evaluated our areas of weakness, we need to prayer-fully ask the Lord to help us overcome what holds us back. If workaholism keeps you enslaved to a job at the risk of your family life or your walk with God, take it to the cross and leave it! If these problems have caused difficulties with the people you care about, make seeking their forgiveness a priority. Now that's the way to prioritize!

WOW!

Prayer Pick-Me-Up

"As a mother of four, I think 'quality time' is a myth. Life does not fit into neat little time packages. You need to be there for your family, church, and work when needed. Often, my priorities are out of balance, but I have learned that daily prayer time needs to come first. Since I work in the city (Chicago), I go to a chapel at lunchtime and pray every day. Occasionally, I skip that prayer time because of a rush project at work or lunch with a friend. I have noticed that my 'lunchtime with God' makes a difference in my ability to handle my rushed schedule and parenting responsibilities. No matter how stressed or discouraged I feel, I always come away from my 'lunchtime with God' with a renewed sense of faith that God will help me handle whatever comes up. Also, I have a close prayer friend with whom I share my concerns. Talking with her and knowing that she is also praying renews me spiritually."
—Linda, Batavia, IL

YOUR PRIORITY LIST

Answer each question below or on a separate sheet of paper. This is your time to be honest before God and to solicit His help to set your priorities in order.

1. Your top three priorities (the activities you give the most time to):

   _____

   _____

   _____

2. What would you change about your life right now concerning the activities that consume most of your time? Would you spend more time or less doing those activities? Why?

CATCH A CLUE

Other Resources

- *First Things First,* **Stephen R. Covey, A. Roger Merrill, Rebecca R. Merrill (New York: Fireside, 1994)**
- *How Now Shall We Live?* **Charles Colson (Wheaton, IL: Tyndale House, 1999).**
- *Celebrate the Family,* **Gary Smalley and John Trent, Ph.D. (Wheaton, IL: Focus on the Family/Tyndale House, 1999).**

3. If you had a "time wish list," how much time would you allot each day to
   - Family?
   - Work?
   - Your church community?
   - Other: _____

4. What will you do this week to show your commitment to
   - Family?
   - Work?
   - Your church community?

5. Obstacles that stand in the way of your spending time with family, keeping productive at work, or being a contributing member of your church body:

Quality Time

WOW!

" 'Quality time' can only happen in the context of 'quantity time.' That's because we can't schedule when a child will have a need or a deep question or be open to discussion and guidance. But 'quantity time' must focus on the family or individual child—being in the same room while I read the paper or watch TV doesn't count.

"My mother suffered from Alzheimer's disease, and my father died first, trying to care for her. When my mother died, my three brothers, one sister, and I were finally able to come to closure and to deal with our grief at losing both parents. At the funeral home, after visitation hours, we, along with our spouses and children, sat and reminisced, especially about Mom. We remembered with joy much about her life; for example, her commitment to Christ and to her family and her great gift of hospitality. My brother Paul remembered seeing her on her knees praying for us kids.

"Later that evening, on the way home, I thought of how I wanted my two girls to remember me, at a similar occasion in the future—my visitation and funeral. I want them to see me as one who loved God, my wife, and children, of course. But one thought overwhelmed me: I want them to remember, 'Dad was there.' Since then, I have tried to be there...for their practices and games and performances and other important events. They won't remember my lectures and only a few of my jokes, but they will remember my presence."
—Dave Veerman

MEANINGFUL LABOR

"What does man gain from all his labor at which he toils under the sun?" (Ecclesiastes 1:3). Have you asked yourself that question lately? If your answer was "Meaningless! Meaningless! . . . Everything is meaningless" in the words of "the Teacher" (Ecclesiastes 1:2), then maybe it's time to give some thought to finding satisfaction in your work. Is that possible? You betcha! So, how do you go about doing that?

ASK GOD TO GIVE YOU A BALANCED VIEW

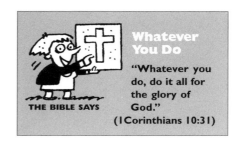

Whatever You Do

"Whatever you do, do it all for the glory of God."
(1 Corinthians 10:31)

THE BIBLE SAYS

Sometimes when we feel that things aren't going our way, we look at life through the lens of our own disappointment. That view colors everything to the point where everything seems "meaningless." We wonder, *How on earth did I ever put up with this job?* When those times come, prayer needs to come as quickly as your next breath. Rather than make a quick decision ("I'll quit and find a better job!"), ask God to help you regain a more balanced view of your work situation. You may find, when your cloudy day turns sunny, that life isn't quite so bad.

SET YOUR MIND ON JESUS

If you're serious about finding satisfaction in what you do, "Set your hearts on things above, where Christ is seated at the right hand of God. Set your minds on things above, not on earthly things" (Colossians 3:1–2). Does this mean walking around your office quoting Scripture and looking pious? Does this mean telling your boss, "I can't fill out my sales report because I have to spend time in meditation?" Noooo. It does mean looking to God to help you find satisfaction in what you do.

Many times, we get caught up in "the rat race": wanting a promotion because Doug has one; wanting to make more money than Suzi; wanting to fulfill a personal agenda that we set because we want to be millionaires by the time we're thirty. Such goals can drain the satisfaction we might feel from a job well done—no matter what that job is. Such goals also keep our eyes focused on "earthly things." Trying to keep up with the Joneses of the workplace is a sure-fire way to drain the satisfaction out of any occupation. That's why we're constantly reminded in Scripture to look to God. Looking to Him helps remind us to be thankful for what He's given us, including meaningful work. Being thankful is one road to satisfaction!

Hard at Work or Hardly Working?

"[I] tried working once, but it didn't work out. Too much like work."
—Steed, one of the lead characters in an episode of *The Avengers*

WOW!

BE JOYFUL

How satisfied is someone who grumbles? Not very, right? Grumbling is one of the fastest routes to dissatisfaction. To take a "detour," consider some advice from Paul, "Whatever is true, whatever is noble, whatever is right, whatever is pure, whatever is lovely, whatever is admirable—if anything is excellent or praiseworthy—think about such things" (Philippians 4:8). As Wrigley's, the chewing gum manufacturer, would say, "Now that's pure satisfaction!"

DO WORK THAT IS SATISFYING TO YOU

Seems obvious, right? Yet judging by the amount of people who claim to hate their jobs, it must not be. Many of us are forced to work out of necessity (rent, food, etc.) with the belief that a paycheck is better than no paycheck. Many times, the opportunities for working in our college fields of study just aren't there. Perhaps we could take lessons from some of the retirees. You've probably seen many happy seniors bagging groceries, smiling at Wal-Mart, or delivering cars to dealerships. Many will tell you that now they are retired, they finally feel free enough to do the kinds of jobs they always wanted.

You don't have to wait until you're sixty-five (or fifty-nine and a half) years old to do that. In fact, *don't* wait until you're retired to at least *try* to find work that satisfies. Make it your mission to search the want ads, go back to school, do an Internet search—whatever is necessary to make a change. Don't forget to pray first!

CATCH A CLUE

True Fulfillment

"Work is truly fulfilling only when it is firmly tied to its moral and spiritual moorings. It is time for the church to reclaim this crucial part of life, restoring a biblical understanding of work and economics."
—Charles Colson in *How Now Shall We Live?*

SECTION 2
BEING A GOOD EMPLOYEE

RELATING TO THE BOSS

Each of us has our own unique personalities and preferences (some of us being quirkier than others). Some like black coffee, others don't like coffee at all. Some like to talk out loud while thinking, others think first and then talk. The same is true of your boss, only his or her personality and preferences carry over into management style. If you want to have a good working relationship with your boss, make it a point to identify specific quirks and preferences. Since that person usually has the power to fire you or give you a raise, it just makes sense to communicate and relate to your boss the way he or she prefers.

Hands-On versus Hands-off Boss
The hands-on boss likes to tightly control what is happening in her department whereas others prefer a hands-off approach. If you report to a hands-on boss, she will be consistently wanting to know what, how, when, where, and why things are happening. So by all means, let her know! Make it a point to involve her in most of your decisions. Keeping the hands-on boss in the dark can be disastrous if she finds out you've been handling something in a way she did not expect or something is happening she didn't know about. At the same time, a hands-off boss can become frustrated if she knows your every thought, project, and decision. She would prefer to delegate the job to you and then only hear from you when it's done or if you need help.

Detailed versus Big Picture Boss
Some bosses are very detail oriented whereas others are more the

give-me-the-big-picture type. If you report to "Mr. Detail," we suggest you keep good documentation of what you're doing and when, whom you've talked to, pending decisions, and ones that have been made. Provide informative reports with plenty of background details and recommended action steps, noting pros and cons of each. If, however, you report to "Mr. Big Picture," he will be bored to tears with a lengthy discourse filled with the research you've done. In this situation, less is better. Briefly report on the bottom line, what's going well, what's not. The whys can be saved for when he asks.

Analyzing versus Free-associating Boss

When making decisions or dealing with issues, some managers like to brainstorm out loud. This free associating calls for you to be able to think on your feet. Just sitting there with a dumb-guy look and your mouth shut is not very impressive. If your boss likes to talk it out, be sure to take good notes. These types of managers usually expect you to pick up the ball and run with it, so you need to remember exactly what was discussed. On the other hand, some bosses would rather do their thinking alone. Rather than making an unannounced visit to his office to share your ideas for the new advertising campaign, he would rather you put your thoughts in writing and then set up a meeting to discuss it after he's had time to give it some thought.

Know Your Audience

WIDE ANGLE

"It took me awhile to realize that my boss was not reading the E-mails and misplacing the reports I was providing him. Being a detailed person myself, I only assumed that he wanted to be as informed as possible about the projects I was working on. I started to sense he trusted my judgment and didn't want to rehash my research. Our working relationship really improved when I began communicating in concise summaries rather than details."
—Marshall, Jackson, Mississippi

FOLLOW DIRECTIONS

Obviously when your boss asks you to do something, you need to do it. But, you must be sure you understand what is expected of you. Getting the job done right the first time always looks better at review time. But sometimes it requires more than simply following steps 1-2-3. To make sure you fully understand what's expected of you, we've listed some tips to help you follow through on your end of the project:

1. Listen carefully to directions and ask questions.

If you hear an unfamiliar term, or are unclear about some aspect of your project or job, don't be afraid to have it clarified. Trust us. It's better to be momentarily uncomfortable as you express your lack of knowledge than to have it clarified for you in a reprimand or pink slip because you did the job completely wrong.

2. Watch body language.

Not only do you need to listen to *what* is being spoken, but also to the manner in which it is presented. "Watching" body language (such as arm movements) and hearing voice inflections, clarifies the verbal message.

3. Take notes.

Not only will this help you remember what was discussed, it looks impressive. You may want to consider using a Day Timer or planner to consolidate your calendar, to-do list, and meeting notes.

4. Recap the specifics.

Don't end a meeting where you have accepted a task without first recapping the specifics with your boss. End your summary with, "Is this what you're expecting?" and be sure to include:

- Overview of the project, task, responsibility
- Urgency/deadline
- Resources available to you, including people, money, time, etc.
- How you are to report progress or problems

REPORT PROGRESS TO YOUR BOSS

It is in your best interest (and your company's) to regularly check in to be sure you're focused on the items that your boss deems most important. The purpose is to avoid being diverted without your boss knowing it. You would certainly hate to be thinking you're going in the right direction with a project and spend a lot of time working on it only to find your boss had other ideas. Depending on your boss's management style, this could be a brief E-mail report, a scheduled meeting, or a weekly lunch.

SCHMOOZING

While you may not want to admit it, schmoozing *is* a successful technique to get along with your boss. Some call it brown-nosing; we like to call it strategic relationship building. Ignore that age-old saying, *Flattery will get you nowhere,* because studies are showing that if two people are both competent at what they do, but one is really good at schmoozing the boss, the one likely to get the raise is the schmoozer. We are not advocating lying, telling your boss how great he or she looks everyday, or implying you should be fake in your relationship. Effective schmoozing is showing genuine interest in your boss. Be social. Take the time to ask him about his personal life, family, and hobbies. Good job performance blended with "strategic relationship building" is an effective combination for relating to your boss.

RELATING TO COWORKERS

Unless you've chosen to live as a hermit, life is filled with relationships. When you were young, you learned how to relate to your siblings and family. As you got older, your world expanded and you had to relate to friends, classmates, teachers, teammates, and roommates. And now that you're in the workplace, you have to relate to your coworkers. Fortunately, relating to coworkers is not much different than relating to anyone else. And if you've ever heard the expression, *everything you know you learned in kindergarten*, it applies here. Relating to your coworkers doesn't require learning some new relationship technique. It's just practical common sense and the same God-honoring approach to relationships you learned when you were young.

Top Five Ways to Irritate Non-Morning People

THE BOTTOM LINE

5. Get in their faces and start talking about your wonderful weekend or evening.
4. After they sit down at their desks, immediately start bombarding them with questions.
3. Cut them off before they reach the coffee machine.
2. Talk really loud.
1. Whistle the tune, "Put On A Happy Face."

1. Smile and say good morning.

Let's face it, some folks are morning people and others are not. You can usually recognize those who are not by their scowls, sullen attitudes, and cranky dispositions. They're the ones either complaining about everything, or cradling their coffee and sending the *Don't talk to me* signal. You know to just stay out of their way. Whether you're a morning person or not, there's no reason you can't start each day out on a positive note. You might find it actually elevates your spirit as well as those around you. So regardless of how you slept last night, greet your coworkers with a smile and say, *"Good morning."* It will create an atmosphere of teamwork and collaboration.

CATCH A CLUE

Five Ways to Thank Coworkers

1. **Give them a gift certificate for a video rental, restaurant, or mall.**
2. **Buy them a sweet treat and place it on their desk as a surprise.**
3. **Send them a thank-you card.**
4. **Publicly recognize them.**
5. **Take them out to lunch.**

2. Say thank you.

Rarely does one person successfully complete a project alone. Generally a whole host of people participates at some level. For instance, a direct mail campaign may involve support staff entering data into a computer or placing mailing labels on each envelope. And yes, while that is "their job," a little recognition helps to improve your working relationship and work environment. So tomorrow, why not give a verbal "thank you" or write an E-mail to recognize others and their input. Let your coworkers know they are appreciated.

3. Listen and keep an open mind.

There are always going to be coworkers who share your views and coworkers who disagree with you. But keep in mind, if everyone had the same opinion and always agreed with each other, no new ideas or strategies would be developed, and the company could become stagnant. So next time you find yourself in disagreement or opposition with a coworker, we don't recommend flying off the handle in a fit of rage or stubbornly ignoring his ideas. Neither of these will improve your working relationship. Instead, genuinely listen to his perspective and try very hard to objectively understand his point of view. If you maintain an open mind, you might realize he has some good ideas, ones that might actually be better than yours! If, on the other hand, you still disagree, state your perspective in a professional, non-threatening way. Use phrases like "This is how I feel" or "I have a different perspective." Avoid phrases like "You always" or "You never." Conclude such dialogues, regardless of the outcome, by thanking him for taking time to share his ideas and stating that you appreciate hearing from him.

4. *Fulfill your commitments.*

Nothing can be more aggravating than when a coworker pledges to do something and doesn't do it. The same is true for you. When you promise to do something, it is imperative that you follow through with your word. Don't be a yes person and say you'll do something just to look good up front, because if you don't get it finished, everyone will be mad later. If you're not sure you can complete a project or assignment, be honest about your concerns and the time frame. Maybe some changes can be made to help you get it done. Completing your end of an assignment keeps your working relationships with coworkers smooth.

5. *Be friendly.*

Nothing improves your working relationship with someone more than being friendly. While we're not advocating becoming best friends with each of your coworkers, do take time to show genuine care about other people and their lives. Ask questions, smile, listen, and look them in the eyes when talking with them. Ignoring people in the coffee room and always keeping to yourself does nothing to build relationships. Being friendly eases tension, and people will enjoy being around you.

6. Be an example.

Our human nature is to treat others as they treat us. If they talk behind our backs, we talk behind theirs. If they refuse to help us out, we refuse them help. It doesn't take an advanced degree to figure out that approach doesn't foster good working relationships. But God calls us to a higher standard. In Luke 6:31, Jesus says that we should, "Do unto others as you would have them do unto you." Don't let circumstances, people, or personalities prevent you from setting an example and maintaining a positive, loving attitude toward your coworkers.

This Little Light of Mine. . .

THE BIBLE SAYS

"You are the light of the world. A city on a hill cannot be hidden. Neither do people light a lamp and put it under a bowl. Instead they put it on its stand, and it gives light to everyone in the house. In the same way, let your light shine before men, that they may see your good deeds and praise your Father in heaven."
(Matthew 5:14–16)

7. Don't be a tattletale.

Nobody likes a tattletale. You won't be very well respected among your coworkers if every time someone does something you don't like or think is mean, you run and tell the boss. For example, if someone isn't doing her job as well as she could or should and it's making more work for you, instead of tattling to the boss to get her in trouble, try going to the coworker directly and resolving the issue. If, on the other hand, the coworker is doing something unethical like stealing or making personal long distance phone calls on the company dime, then by all means, say something to the boss.

DEALING WITH A DIFFICULT COWORKER

What if you're following all our recommendations and there is still a coworker whom you don't get along with? You know, the one who seems to have made it her mission to make your life difficult and uncomfortable? Well, as much as we'd like to say just quit and look for another job, we know that won't help. No job is perfect. There is someone like this at every job. Since running away is not an option, try the following methods to deal with your difficult coworker.

- Don't stoop to her level. When you give up trying to improve the relationship, matters will only get worse. Continue to be friendly as possible, listen with an open mind, and be an example. In time, she may come around.

You've Gotta Love 'Em

THE BIBLE SAYS "Love your enemies, do good to those who hate you, bless those who curse you, pray for those who mistreat you." (Luke 5:27–28)

- Don't focus on her personality. Instead of nit-picking and continually coming up with things about her that drive you crazy, focus on how your skills can work together to get the job done.
- Pray for the coworker and the situation. You are not alone. Ask God to help you deal with the situation and show kindness to the person.

- Address the issue. If the person is so hard to deal with that it is inhibiting your production, try talking with the person about the situation. Don't come across with a confrontational attitude, and be sure to use the statement "I feel" instead of "You always."

INTRA-OFFICE DATING

For some, the thrill of love in the workplace conjures up romantic illusions of flowers waiting on the desk, intimate lunch dates, giggling by the water cooler, seeing that person all day, and possibly marriage. But are work romances really ideal? The intra-office relationship is a widely talked about and debated topic. Some experts advise against any romance in the workplace while others suggest that intra-office dating can be successful. Either way, relationships in the workplace should be handled delicately. If the romantic feelings are not mutual, a breakup happens or unwanted advances turn into harassment. Problems tend to mass produce themselves and the fireworks fly. And it's usually not the Fourth of July. This section will not attempt to recommend whether or not you should have a work romance but provides some guidelines and issues to consider.

PITFALLS TO CONSIDER

1. Difficulty working together

Unlike in school where you basically just coexist in the same environment with your romantic interests, on the job you actually have to work with your coworkers to get a job done. This often requires collaborating and making decisions together. What happens when you disagree with your romantic counterpart? What if you end up vying for the same promotion? What if you're in direct competition for sales or perks? If you're emotionally involved with a coworker, it can make working together much more difficult.

2. The socializing dilemma

Coworkers who are dating may sometimes spend more time socializing on company time than focusing on their jobs. This can result in being disliked by other coworkers, reprimanded, demoted, or even fired. Or if you are trying to keep your relationship a secret from the other staff, you may be spending a lot of mental energy on how others are perceiving your relationship or whether you're socializing too much, making you less productive. Above all, remember you're both professionals in the work-place, so act accordingly.

3. Ethical challenges

Dating your boss or someone who reports directly to you can create ethical challenges. The boss might find it difficult to not show favoritism and be more lenient toward a boyfriend or girlfriend than others. Or the situation may be reversed. The boss may be more strict with his "ex." The boss walks a fine line between satisfying his responsibilities at work and expectations in his dating relationship, particularly when it comes time for performance review, raises, bonuses, or promotions.

WIDE ANGLE

Dating the Boss

"I dated my boss at my last job. We were able to maintain a professional working relationship, but it was very hard. I wouldn't recommend it, and I wouldn't do it again. No one ever confronted me, but I always worried people would find out and judge me harshly. The pressure got to be too great, so I switched jobs, but shortly afterwards, we broke up."
—Victoria, Wenatchee, Washington

4. Coworker response

You have two options in handling your romantic relationship. You can either keep it a secret from your coworkers, or you can be open and honest with everyone. As for the former, let's face it, no one can keep a secret for long. Usually you end up telling your best coworker friend in strict confidence requiring all sorts of pledges and promises that he or she will tell no one else. But as soon as someone else suspects and asks about it, he or she will spill the beans, then that person tells someone else, and pretty soon, the cat is out of the bag. But if you decide to be open with your coworkers about your relationship, be prepared for teasing, gossip, and possible anger or jealousy. Life could get pretty difficult.

5. The breakup blues

No one enters a relationship expecting that it's going to end. Your hopes and dreams are that the romantic feelings will go on forever. But then reality hits, and you find this intra-office dating thing isn't cracked up to be what you thought. Where are the flowers on your desk every

WOW!

Every Single Day

"I dated a coworker for about eight months, but ended up breaking it off. After that he was very difficult to work with and made my life miserable. He would snap at me in front of our coworkers and get angry at me for petty things. I tried to be friendly with him, but he wouldn't even give me the time of day. I just wanted to avoid him, but he was someone I had to deal with every single day."
—Angela, Appleton, Wisconsin

morning? And since you started dating, you've only had one romantic lunch date. And what about the way he greeted you this morning? Was it because he is mad at you or is he just having a bad day? While a few intra-office relationships end in marriage, most crash and burn, leaving a painful trail behind them. Before entering one of these relationships, consider the ramifications of a breakup. You still have to see this person every day. You might still have to work on projects and make decisions together. He or she could share things about you with other coworkers that you don't want to be public knowledge. If the breakup isn't mutual, there could still be anger and hurt that comes out in unprofessional ways. Our point? Be prepared for the aftermath at the end of the intra-office romance.

COMPANY POLICY

Before you give the key to your heart away to a coworker, first find out if your company has a policy about dating in the workplace. Some organizations expressly prohibit intra-office dating relationships. And while that may be difficult to define and enforce, and you're tempted to sneak, just get those thoughts out of your head. If your company has such a policy, it would be much better for your résumé to quit your job and then start the relationship than to be fired over it. Make sure to check your employee handbook to see if such a policy exists before asking out that cute blond in accounting. However, most organizations do not have such a strict dating policy. In this case, check what precedent your company has set in the past with other work romances. And don't use the "grapevine" to get this information. Rather, go directly to your human resources manager. He will give you the straight scoop and should honor your request to keep your inquiry confidential.

UNSTOPPABLE ROMANCE

You've considered the pitfalls, you know your company policy, but you still have feelings for each other that refuse to be ignored. Feeling a bit like Romeo and Juliet? Let's consider your options. Fortunately, they are better than pretending to drink poison or killing yourself, but we have to admit, you are in a difficult position. In fact, it is likely that to continue dating, one of you may need to leave your employer. So take some time to honestly consider the ramifications of breaking up or staying together. Will your career or your relationship suffer? While discreetly hiding your relationship may work for awhile, it can't be a secret forever. Pretty soon someone will notice that look in your eyes or your inside jokes. Instead, be up front and present your situation to management. Together you can work out a solution that meets everyone's needs and expectations. But if that isn't possible and continuing the relationship is important, you may be the one finding a new job.

WHEN YOU DON'T WANT TO GO OUT

With some people, you just feel that spark. You want things to work out between you. You're willing to put your job on the line for love. But other times it's just the opposite. Someone asks you out, and you feel no fire, no spark, and there's no matchstick in sight. So how do you give him the signal that you're not interested without hurting his feelings?

CATCH A CLUE

Top 5 Worst Ways to Say No to a Coworker Date:

5. I would, but I already have a date with Jim in finance.
4. Oh, sorry, that's the night I wash my hair.
3. Hmm, uh, you know, I've got that thing. . .
2. You know, I just don't think I can fit you in.
1. The thought of going out with you makes my skin crawl.

- Watch your tone. Don't just blurt out, *NO WAY!,* unless you want to see him slink back to his desk.

- Be firm. Don't be wishy-washy and leave the door open for a later invitation. "You know, I really don't think so. Gee, maybe another time," sends mixed signals and is an open door for future invitations.
- Don't lie. It never works when you make up an excuse. "You know, I can't. I've got a funeral to go to," just sets you up to get caught in your own deceit.
- Remember your manners. Politely say, "No thanks, I'm not interested." And leave it at that. You don't need an excuse, and you've closed the door to future invitations.

SEXUAL HARASSMENT

Remember the famous senate hearings involving Clarence Thomas and Anita Hill? Her accusations of his alleged sexual harassment almost stood in the way of him filling a position on the Supreme Court. Since then, sexual harassment has become a hot topic, and specific guidelines have been set up by the EEOC (Equal Employment Opportunity Commission) to control and minimize sexual harassment in the workplace. The EEOC, the government's primary tool for fighting job discrimination, defines sexual harassment as any unwelcome sexual advances, requests for sexual favors, and other verbal or physical conduct of sexual nature when:

1) submitting or refusing to submit to that conduct is used as a basis for any decision affecting an individual's employment or status, or
2) that conduct has the purpose or effect of creating an intimidating, hostile, or offensive working environment or
3) that conduct is used by a supervisor to discriminate against an employee.

Sexual harassment is a highly sensitive subject. What one person considers to be casual flirting, another person might take as an offensive comment. So let it be said, you must watch what you say. On the other hand, don't tolerate someone's unwelcome sexual advances or comments because you're embarrassed or intimidated. Sexual harassment is a serious offense. If you feel you have been subjected to it in any way, shape, or form, report the conduct to your human resource manager. If you are coming up against a brick wall at your company, contact the nearest EEOC department for assistance. Call 1-800-669-EEOC.

THE BOTTOM LINE

Tell Someone

"There was a guy at my company that kept asking me out on a date, but I usually gave some dumb reason why I couldn't go. He frequently told me how cute I was, but when I finally told him flat out I didn't want to go out, he started directing his comments toward my body. I felt really uncomfortable and kept it to myself for a time but then decided to tell my boss. After I explained my situation, I found out he had done the same thing to two other women at the company. Shortly after, the man was fired."
—Alison, Washington D.C.

THE DAMAGE OF GOSSIP

You're standing in the coffee room minding your own business when she comes in. After pouring her coffee, she checks the room for others and whispers, "Did you hear about Sheila's new boyfriend?" And before you can make a run for the door, she dives into details you'd think only Sheila and her boyfriend would know. Inevitably, there is at least one gossip in every workplace. It's almost as if there was some unwritten rule that each company has to fill a gossip quota. Our point? You can't get away from gossip. Unless you work alone, you are going to run into gossip, so you've got to be prepared to deal with it and the gossiper.

HEART CHECK

Your world at work is the common denominator between you and your coworkers. So it's easy to let the people, their lives, and the day-to-day events become the fodder for gossip. Although it's tempting to listen a little here and talk a little there just to keep your ear to the ground on company current events, the Bible specifically refers to the gossiper as problematic and gossip as a sin. "A gossip separates close friends" (Proverbs 16:28). "A gossip betrays a confidence but a trustworthy man keeps a secret" (Proverbs 11:13). In Romans 1:29–30, gossip is linked with other sins that those who have turned away from God are involved in. "They have become filled with every kind of wickedness, evil, greed and depravity. They are full of envy, murder, strife, deceit and malice. They are gossips, slanderers,

God-haters, insolent, arrogant and boastful. . ." Whew! That is not a pretty picture! But it's not just a matter of saying to yourself, "I won't gossip anymore," it's a matter of heart. In Luke 6:25, Jesus says, "The good man brings good things out of the good stored up in his heart, and the evil man brings evil things out of the evil stored up in his heart. For out of the overflow of his heart his mouth speaks." So before opening your mouth, check your heart and your motives.

GET AWAY

Do you ever think to yourself, *Hey, I'm not the one to start any gossip or rumors? It is sort of fun to keep up on what's going on in the company. It's not wrong to just listen*. If you have this attitude, beware. It is so easy to get pulled in. Pretty soon, you're asking questions, getting more details, and thinking about other people in ways you might not have before. And inevitably, you will tell someone else. No matter how tight you lock your lips and throw away the key, there always seems to be a

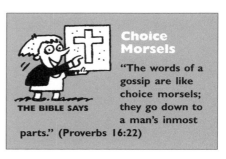

Choice Morsels

THE BIBLE SAYS "The words of a gossip are like choice morsels; they go down to a man's inmost parts." (Proverbs 16:22)

spare or you remember where you threw it. Take our advice and avoid the gossips, or you'll become one yourself.

FAUX FRIEND

If someone appears to be your friend but is talking *to* you about someone else and his business, it's highly likely that he is talking *about* you and your business to someone else. People who gossip will gossip about anything or anybody. So unless you don't mind being the topic of the break room, be careful about what you share with that person. Unfortunately, no one is immune from gossip. Even if they know nothing about your life, those who gossip will still find something to wag their tongues about—and you may be the main topic.

DEALING WITH GOSSIP

Sometimes it seems like the law of nature that the harder you try not to gossip the more those around you are gossiping. So if you find yourself in the predicament where someone is trying to fill your ear about someone else, kindly tell her you don't want to hear it and you don't need to know that person's business. Remember, it's important to say it kindly. You're trying to set an example, not make enemies.

Getting Burned

CATCH A CLUE

"Once I told in confidence a coworker, whom I thought was a friend, that my husband and I were thinking about getting pregnant. And then, a few weeks later, I overheard her talking about my situation to someone else. Was I ever mad! But I should have known better. She had shared some things with me about other people that I probably shouldn't have known, but I guess I thought we were better friends than that. Guess I should've seen it coming."
—Joreen, Rupert, Idaho

IS THERE ANY GOOD GOSSIP?

Some people use the guise of "We need to pray for so and so because. . ." and then launch into juicy details about something happening in someone's life. Don't use prayer as an excuse for sharing personal information about someone else. This is still considered gossip. Fortunately God already knows the details, making it possible to pray for the person without knowing the situation.

QUESTIONS TO ASK YOURSELF

1. What do I do when someone starts talking to me about someone else's personal life?

THE BOTTOM LINE

How To Diffuse Gossipers:

- **Offer them something to eat so they'll use their mouths another way. Better yet, stuff their mouths so they can't talk.**
- **When they take a breath, start a new topic. Ask them about themselves.**
- **Continue working; hopefully they'll get the hint that they should be, too.**
- **Pretend you're not listening, and don't.**
- **Politely explain that you don't want to hear it.**

2. What is my motive for gossiping?

3. What is my new response to gossip going to be?

4. How can I encourage my coworkers not to gossip?

5. How can I make it up to someone whom I've hurt by gossiping?

OTHER GREAT BOOKS TO READ (BESIDES THIS ONE)

Business by the Book: The Complete Guide to Biblical Principles for the Workplace by Larry Burkett.
This book encourages readers to have integrity in the workplace rather than follow the crowd because "everybody else is doing it."

Company Manners: How to Behave in the Workplace in the 90s by Lois Wyse.
This book separates the do's from the don'ts of business conduct in the 90s. Includes sections on sexual harassment, family leave, flextime, etc.

Executive Etiquette in the New Workplace by Marjabelle Young Stewart and Marian Faux.
Covering dozens of issues, such as the correct way to ask a colleague to refrain from smoking and the proper method of addressing a CEO (first name or not?), this guide to corporate conduct will help launch anyone's career.

I Hate My Boss: How to Survive and Get Ahead When Your Boss Is a Tyrant, Control Freak, or Just Plain Crazy by Bob Weinstein.
Whew! What a title! With many useful anecdotes, the author demonstrates

the pros and cons of various strategies for dealing with your boss.

Make Yourself Memorable: Winning Strategies to Help You Make a Great Impression on Your Boss, Your Coworkers, Your Customers and Everyone Else! by Stephanie G. Sherman, V. Clayton Sherman.
Includes guidelines for creating an impact on others and improving business relationships.

Problem People at Work: The Essential Survival Guide for Dealing with Bosses, Coworkers, Employees, and Outside Clients by Marilyn Wheeler.
This helpful guide identifies four key "communication styles," offers help in recognizing one's own style, and gives insight into how to understand any problem person in the workplace.

The Joy of Work: Dilbert's Guide to Finding Happiness at the Expense of Your Coworkers by Scott Adams.
This is not a collection of Dilbert cartoons but a humorous guide to surviving the corporate life.

Type Talk at Work/How the 16 Personality Types Determine Your Success on the Job by Otto Kroeger, Janet M. Theusen.
These authors take the Myers-Briggs Type Indicator test to the workplace and show how people can handle personal and personnel matters.

Work It Out: Clues for Solving People Problems at Work by Sandra Krebs Hirsh, Hane A.G. Kise.
Two personality type experts demonstrate the effects of different personalities at work and how to facilitate more effective work relationships.

SECTION 3
RULES OF THE ROAD

PRESENTING REPORTS

You have spent countless hours researching, analyzing, brainstorming, documenting, and working hard to thoroughly complete an important project. Now the time has come to present your findings and recommendations to upper management. But don't let all your hard work go down the drain with a poor presentation. Whether you're preparing a written report or need to provide a multimedia presentation, there are ways to make sure your report is professionally and meaningfully presented.

PREPARING A WRITTEN REPORT

Though you could probably create a one-hundred-page document with all the details of your research and analysis, the reason you're writing a report is to *summarize* the key points. Keep in mind your readers can't devote all day to reading your report, so include only the necessary research details. If you absolutely must include

THE BOTTOM LINE

The Executive Summary:

Include in your executive summary:

a) a statement why the report is being written.

b) a statement or bullet point list of key information or research.

c) a statement or bullet point list of your conclusions or recommendations.

lengthy details, document them in the form of an appendix. Using bullet points or the outline format reduces the length of your report by forcing you to only use words or phrases rather than complete sentences. Most often, a one-page report has more impact than a ten-page report. In the situations where your report will exceed three to five pages, we recommend that you begin your report with an executive summary, an overview of your report.

Not only does the executive summary help prepare your reader for the rest of the report, it may be the only thing some people have time to read. For longer reports (seven or more pages) use a table of contents summarizing key sections of the report and what page number they can be found on.

Here are some other ideas to make sure your report looks professional and is as helpful as possible.

- Date it. People don't want to look at an old report and wonder when it was written.
- Sign it. Recipients want to know who prepared the report.
- Use page numbers. It's hard to be reviewing a ten-page report with someone else and have no point of reference where you are in the document.
- Use appropriate font and point size. Don't reduce your font to dinky letters just to fit it all on one page.
- Use a common software program. Make sure your word processing software is one your recipients use. Attaching files to an E-mail is a popular way to distribute reports. Using a different software program will prevent them from reading your hard work.
- Use graphics. When appropriate, spice up your report with a pie chart or bar graph. Inserted in the right place, it could have more impact than a summary. Most spreadsheets can quickly create some nice graphics.

PRESENTING YOUR REPORT

Did you know that speaking in front of people is actually feared more than death? Unbelievable as it sounds, people would rather die than speak in public. There's just something dreadful about getting up in front of others all alone and risking making a fool of yourself. *What if I forget what I'm supposed to say? What if I trip over my words? What if I don't make any sense?* All these are common fears about speaking in front of others. Fortunately there are times when a written report will do, but at some point in your career, you'll have to present a report at work. To help make your presentation a success, we've outlined some tips to guide you.

Speak Clearly
What did you say? It's imperative that you speak in a concise manner using only the amount of words needed to make your point, or people will get lost in the muddle. Know the key points you want to make and choose your words carefully. (This is best done ahead of time.) And don't forget to leave out the "uh's" and "um's." While they are only verbal pauses, they can be distracting to the listener.

Speak Slowly
We know that all you want to do is get your presentation over with and sit down. But talking a mile a minute often causes you to stumble over your words or slur your speech, causing confusion and misinterpretation among your listeners. So unless you want to get back up and reclarify yourself, speak slowly the first time.

Be Confident
We realize that telling you to be confident is like saying to a tree, "OK, now be a rock." It's very, very difficult. But if you have done your homework and preparation, you've won half the battle. Now it's just a matter of communicating your message to the audience. So take a few deep breaths, relax, smile, and speak clearly and slowly. Still not feeling confident? Fake it.

Be Comfortable

Ever feel like a bumbling clown when you stand up to talk? All of the sudden your arms become these long, gangly things that just get in the way. You feet feel ten sizes too big, and your hands don't seem to have a job, so you stuff them in your pockets. But don't get too hung up on whether you should or shouldn't pace the floor or use your hands while talking. Just do what comes naturally.

Look At The Audience

More often than not, presenters tend to get up on center stage, read their notes and sit down as quickly as possible. Let us suggest that if at all possible, avoid reading and instead make eye

A Word about Media Style

CATCH A CLUE

Don't overdo the multimedia bit. Remember, you want the audience to know what you have done, not merely how you presented it. If the bells and whistles from your multimedia equipment overshadow your substance, you have gone to far. These aids should enhance your work, not overshadow it.

contact with the audience as you speak. Just as you want your audience to be interested in your presentation, they want you to be interested in them. Looking at them will also guide your talk. If you sense a drop in interest, get the audience involved by asking a question either directed at the group or to an individual.

Use Visual Aids

If you have the equipment, use an overhead projector. But if you have the equipment *and* the know-how, use a multimedia slide show. It's very impressive. The slides should be in bullet point format so the audience can read the slide while you elaborate on each point.

Hint: Always practice the slide show first to make sure it flows together. And always be prepared with a backup in case the computer doesn't work or your light bulb burns out in the overhead projector. Our suggestion— print your slide show or transparency so you can distribute hard copies if needed.

E-MAIL CODES OF CONDUCT

Can you even remember what you did before E-mail? You either had to lick a stamp or play phone tag till the cows came home. Now E-mail is a way of life in corporate America, and there are good reasons why. It is an extremely effective way to communicate both internally with coworkers and externally with customers or vendors. File attachments greatly reduce the time and cost to deliver documents in printed form (a.k.a. snail mail), and if managed properly, E-mail can help you better organize important documents and communication without the bulk and limitations of traditional paper and file folders. But before you get head over heels, E-mail does have its downsides. Unfortunately, it is not totally private. Systems administrators have access to your E-mail account for maintenance or problem solving purposes, and E-mail messages can easily be forwarded. So it's necessary to be careful about what you put in print, particularly what you say about others. Not that *you* would say anything bad about anyone!

NETIQUETTE

While users can customize their E-mail to reflect their own individual styles, there are some recommended E-mail codes of conduct (a.k.a. netiquette) that should be followed.

- ***State your message in a concise, professional way.***
  People don't have time to read through an overly long E-mail. Try to focus the E-mail on one specific topic and use a meaningful subject title.

- *Follow traditional business letter format, especially the use of upper- and lower-case letters.*

  Writing an E-mail in ALL CAPITAL LETTERS is annoying to read, and this practice is often called SHOUTING. So if you're new to E-mail, don't send a message to your boss in all caps because you think it looks neat. He'll think you're shouting at him! Likewise, writing an E-mail in all lower-case letters gives the appearance that you are in too much of a hurry.

  Hot Water

  "I'm the sort of person who speaks my mind, but it got me in hot water one day. A coworker of mine wasn't cooperating, so I shot off an E-mail that was misinterpreted. It was then forwarded to my boss who called me in for an explanation. Now I make sure I think twice before I hit 'Send'."
  —Jared, Ottawa, Ontario

  WOW!

  Be sure to capitalize words only to highlight an important point. In fact, a better way to make a point is to surround a word with *Asterisks.*

- *Always include your signature at the end of your message.*

  This is necessary particularly if you are sending an E-mail to someone outside your office. Your signature should include:
  a) your name and title
  b) your company name
  c) your E-mail address
  d) your phone number
  e) your address (optional)

- **Use spell check.**
  For goodness sakes, don't go to the trouble of preparing an E-mail only to include misspelled words. It looks very unprofessional.

- **Review the list of recipients.**
  Before clicking "Send Now," make sure you've included everyone who should receive the message, and think twice to consider if everyone *needs* to receive it. You don't want to gain a reputation of including everyone in all your E-mail correspondence—remember the boy who cried "Wolf!"?

- **Limit the sarcasm.**
  Be extremely careful about putting a sarcastic comment in an E-mail. Without face-to-face communication, the recipient may not know whether you're serious or kidding. When using humor in your E-mail, denote it with the typographical equivalent of a smiley face (:-). Turn your head sideways to the left and you'll see it.

- **Watch for viruses.**
  Some E-mail and E-mail attachments can include a virus intended to harm your computer. So it is a good policy to delete unsolicited E-mail even before you open/read them. Routinely virus-scan your system, particularly before you download an E-mail attachment.

CUBICLE CULTURE

These days real offices with doors and drywall are usually saved for those who hold high positions within a company. So chances are very good that if you work in an office building, your desk area is a cubicle where the only thing separating you from the cube dweller next door are those paper-thin, four feet high, moveable walls. These walls define each person's little nook and create an atmosphere with its own lifestyle and culture. If you are new to the workforce, there are some cultural norms that you need to be aware of.

PRIVACY ISSUES

Even if you walk into your cubicle and feel like you have a bit of privacy, remember that the only thing separating you from the next person is a thin bit of fabric and metal. Keep in mind, these are not the most soundproof of walls. So if you don't want the company gossip to know your secrets, don't share them in your cubicle. And be careful about what you say on the phone. While your neighbor may not be deliberately eavesdropping, sometimes overhearing your conversation is inevitable. Take a tip from the guy who's cubicle was next to "Eagle Ears":

"No matter how quiet I tried to whisper on the phone, my coworker in the cubicle next to me was always listening. The amazing thing was that she never made a secret about it. Once after quietly deciding with my girlfriend where to go to dinner, I said good-bye, and then Eagle Ears commented through the wall that she liked that restaurant and thought we had made a good choice!" —Kent, Boston, Massachusetts

This brings up another point—talking through the cubicle walls. Even though it's obvious how thin the walls are, take the time to get up and walk next door if you need to discuss something. Don't just strike up a conversation through the cubicle wall. The other person might be deeply involved in a project, working on something different than you, or not even there.

Here's another quote from Kent. (Poor guy! We're not sure how he ever got any work done!)

"Frequently my coworker in the cubicle next door (a.k.a. Eagle Ears) would start talking to me about a customer she had just gotten off the phone with or ask me a question about something. Even though I found it annoying, those around me said it was even more distracting when she rambled on and I wasn't at my desk." —Kent, Boston, Massachusetts

THE BOTTOM LINE

No More Mr. Nice Guy

"For awhile my cubicle was next to the copy machine. And since my walls were low, people trying to be nice would say hi and frequently start a up conversation with me. I hardly got any work done and finally asked to be moved."
—**Derek, Eugene, Oregon**

Some cubicles have walls that are only four feet high, making visual privacy impossible. Not only does this limit privacy, it can be very distracting. If you work in this type of environment, be sure not to stare at people as you walk by their desks or feel the need to make small talk with them if they look up. Just pretend a wall separates you and go about your business.

ENTERING SOMEONE'S CUBICLE

With no door to knock on, there is a whole new etiquette to entering someone's "office."

Since each person and work environment is different, we recommend being sensitive to each coworker's personality. If he is the sort of person who hates interruptions, try calling first or E-mailing to set up a time to meet. Other people don't mind you dropping by or stopping to talk whenever you need to. But if you do drop by, check to see if the person is wearing a telephone headset. If so, make sure she isn't talking on the phone or you'll interrupt her.

Four Worst Ways to Enter Someone's Cubicle

WIDE ANGLE

4. Saying, "Hey! Hey! Hey!"
3. Knocking the pattern, "Shave and a haircut, two bits."
2. Tap him on the shoulder when he's not looking.
1. Stand behind him until he senses your presence and turns around.

DECORATING

While you do spend a lot of time in your office, keep in mind that your cubicle is *not* your home away from home, and while how you decorate is a reflection of your style and taste, don't forget, you're still in a professional environment. To help take the fear out of decorating your cubicle, we've provided some guidelines for what's not appropriate.

- *Hanging revealing, or sexy posters, pictures, or calendars such as the* **Sports Illustrated** *swimsuit calendar*

  Come on, this is not your bachelor pad.

- *Hiring an interior decorator*

  There's really no need to call in Martha Stewart to coordinate colors and fabrics. While we've seen *House Beautiful,* we have yet to see a magazine called *Cubicle Beautiful.*

- **Creating the wall of fame**
  While it's nice to have some family photos, or even of just the dog, limit them to a few. It's distracting to you and others if your entire wall or desk gets filled with pictures. You're not creating a cubicle scrapbook.

- **Decorating with fancy and expensive objects**
  Save the Monet and Italian vase for when you have the "real" office. You're not trying to create the cubicle of the rich and famous.

- **Overdoing the sports memorabilia**
  While it's great to cheer for your favorite sports team, don't bring every pennant, program, cap, jersey, pompon, mug, stuffed animal, and poster that you own to your office. You're not the designated cubicle fan club.

Wondering how in the world you should decorate your office after all that? Remember, it's a reflection of who you are. Just keep the items to a minimum. We recognize that these are guidelines for most offices. The "decorating protocol" may vary from business to business depending on occupation and direct customer contact.

SHARING A CUBICLE

Some of you might not have the luxury of having your very own cubicle, but actually share space with someone else. With this comes a whole host of issues, but our best advice is to treat your cube-mate as you would your roommate.

- ***Keep your space clean.***
  Nothing is worse than having a messy roommate, unless you yourself are organizationally-challenged. And if you are, keep in mind that a messy space seems smaller than when it's clean. Pick up a few things, and you might find you actually have two feet more desk space than you thought!

- ***Don't hog office supplies.***
  What could be more bothersome than when the shared stapler, tape, Kleenex, and post-it notes are hidden in your cube-mate's desk? Extend him the courtesy of keeping shared office items in a general place.

- ***Avoid interruptions.***
  You might be the best of buddies, and no matter how much you like to talk, interruptions are distracting when you're trying to work. So save your comments and conversation for breaks and lunchtime. Your time at work is best spent working.

- ***Allow privacy.***
  Privacy in a shared cubicle is almost nonexistent. But there will be times when your cube-mate will need some time to herself. Be sensitive if she is having a bad day, just got chewed out by the boss, or needs a moment to make an important phone call.

ANNOYING HABITS TO AVOID

Certain behaviors are acceptable in some countries but not acceptable in others. For instance, it is customary and acceptable in France to burp at the dinner table. But we all know that for Americans, that is poor etiquette. The same is true within cubicle culture. There are certain behaviors you should avoid. And since we want to make sure that you are not the object of your coworker's loathing and anger, be sure to avoid:

- **Whistling**
  Nothing lifts the spirit more than whistling a happy tune unless you're the one who can't get away from it. Whistling at your desk only annoys others and breaks their concentration, so save it for after hours.

- **Clipping your nails**
  We do advocate good grooming habits, but again it's the sound that is so irritating. That *clip, clip, clip* is very distracting.

- **Breaking wind**
  Rather than submitting your coworkers to the gas chamber, please have the courtesy to hold it or go to the restroom.

- **Listening to loud music through headphones**
  Yes, some companies actually allow their employees to wear head-phones while working. If your company is one, extend the cube dweller next door some peace and quiet and turn the volume down.

EXECUTIVE ETIQUETTE

Just as every culture has its own set of etiquette, so office culture has its own. If you're new to the work force or changing jobs, it's a good idea to understand your new environment and how you should act. You've probably heard the saying, "When in Rome, do as the Romans do." Well it definitely applies here. When in the office, do as the executives do. To make sure you fully understand the rules, we've compiled some helpful hints to make sure you make a smooth transition rather than ruffle some feathers.

First Name Basis

Before calling your boss by his first name or some nickname you made up, wait for him to tell you whether to call him by his first name. If your boss didn't extend you this courtesy (maybe it slipped his mind), wait to find out what your coworkers are calling him. But if you want to be on the safe side (always a wise choice), use Mr. or Mrs. or Ms. until you are told otherwise.

WOW!

There's Always an Exception

"I never knew what to call the teacher I student taught for in college. He never said to call him by his first name, and since he was only about five years older than me, it seemed awkward to call him Mr. Gabriele. So I started calling him Coach, and it stuck. Now that I'm a teacher at that school, I still call him Coach!"
—John, Winfield, Illinois

MEETING MANNERS

Meetings are not like the parties you had in grade school where it became sort of a free-for-all with food. This is much more serious business, so keep in mind when attending a meeting:

- Don't bring food unless it is accepted.
- Don't show up without something to take notes.
- No dozing. You can catch up on sleep later.
- Don't interrupt the boss.

Show Respect

Even if you don't agree with someone or your personalities are polar opposites, show respect for your superiors and their positions. Treat them with the kind of courtesy you would your parents or your grandparents.

Think Before You Speak

"I was participating in an important meeting with the company president and our biggest customer when my coworker peeked his head in to tell us he needed the conference room in fifteen minutes. Needless to say, the president's face said it all."
—**Bob, Omaha, Nebraska**

WOW!

DRESS CODE

Even if you're allowed to wear jeans, be sure not to wear your Saturday work jeans. And remember, it's casual wear, not lounge wear, so look respectable.

BREAK ROOM CARDINAL RULES

5. No matter how much of a rush you're in (or how lazy you are), don't leave the coffeepot empty without making a new pot, unless, of course, it's almost the end of the day.

4. Don't leave the pot turned on if there is only a teeny-tiny bit of coffee left. It will scorch the bottom. And you don't want to be responsible for that, do you?

3. Don't take the last ice cube without refilling the trays with water.

2. Don't forget about your food and leave it in the refrigerator for weeks. We're not doing a penicillin experiment here.

And the number one cardinal rule is:

1. Don't eat anyone else's food unless you have permission. There is nothing more aggravating than to be looking forward all afternoon to the piece of chocolate cake you brought from home and then realizing that someone else has already eaten it!

CATCH A CLUE

Refrigerator Contents

Open a refrigerator in any office and we bet it contains:

1. Moldy bread
2. Two-year-old condiments
3. Last week's dinner leftovers
4. Today's lunch
5. Sour milk
6. Shriveled up fruit
7. Blue cheese that used to be cheddar
8. Expired creamer
9. Empty pizza box
10. At least one unidentifiable item

NO-NO'S

Don't sneak out of the office early without permission. Trust us, people notice. Don't make personal calls on the company dime. Use your calling card if it's an emergency or wait until you get home. Don't take paper and pens home from work. That's called stealing. And don't bring pets or kids to the office. Wait until a Friday afternoon or a holiday.

BE AN EXAMPLE

If you're wearing one of those "WWJD" bracelets (What Would Jesus Do?), no one cares if you're not living it. Either take the bracelet seriously and live like Jesus did or take it off.

PREPARING FOR YOUR REVIEW

Oh, the dreaded performance reviews. They are often a source of great stress for those in the work force. Questions loom: Did I do a good job? What will the company expect from me next year? Will I get a good raise? Ironically, your performance review should not be approached with such questions. It is not a time for you to sit and listen to your boss reflect on the last year and then pat you on the back or boot your behind. Instead, be prepared to share your own thoughts on your performance, goals, and salary. But to do this, you need to be preparing for your review on an ongoing basis throughout the year. Then several weeks before the actual review, provide your boss with an agenda of items you want to discuss at the meeting. Since this is your annual opportunity to address salary, other non-monetary compensation issues, like. . .and to consider your future growth and opportunity, don't take this opportunity lightly. Start getting prepared!

THROUGHOUT THE YEAR

Don't treat your performance appraisal like the New Year's resolutions that get thrown in a drawer somewhere to lay unopened until next January first. We'll give you a moment to dig through your desk or files. Instead, through-out the year, you should regularly take out and review last year's perfor-mance appraisal. What were the items that were considered your "weaknesses" or given a low performance rating last year? Are you taking the necessary steps in your day-to-day activities to improve on these items? If so, document and archive these improvements to refer to later. What goals were set for you this year? Will you realistically meet or beat these goals? If not, is there a legitimate reason why? If, for example, you are given new responsibilities midyear that impact preset objectives, clearly document and communicate that with your supervisor so it doesn't cause you to look bad at the end of the year. And also throughout the year, keep close watch on other employment opportunities. Check newspapers, the Internet, and talk with friends/contacts about opportunities that match your background and skill set. Keep and archive your findings so you have facts about your market value.

WIDE ANGLE

Establishing Your Market Value

To earn more money, you have to show your company that your market value is actually greater than your current salary. To do this:

- **Find out what the market is willing to compensate a person with similar experience, tenure, skills, and credentials.**
- **Network business colleagues, talk with professional associations, and review trade magazines to find out what others in similar jobs earn.**
- **Contact human resources departments and ask for the range of compensation typically offered to candidates like you.**
- **Check the Worldwide Web. Try CareerPath.com, CompGeo On-line, JobSmart Salary Surveys, and U.S. News And World Report's Estimated Starting Salaries. Technology professionals will find useful information at Pencom 1998 Interactive Salary Survey and SalaryMaster.com.**

TWO TO THREE MONTHS BEFORE REVIEW TIME

Take some time now to compile your accomplishments into a meaningful, concise memo. Match accomplishments with personal and corporate goals. Communicate in this memo how you have generated value for the

company. Think through specific issues you want to cover at your review.
- Based upon your research, is a salary increase merited?
- Do you have interests in new responsibilities within your organization?
- Do you have questions about where management sees you in the next one, two, or three years?

Formulate these issues into a meeting agenda and submit this information to your supervisor, indicating that you want to make the most out of your review and that is why you're providing information in advance. This helps your boss know your expectations and gives him a chance to prepare accordingly. (Plus, it just looks good!) If you are seeking a specific salary increase, you will want to submit that request and your research findings now. Waiting until your review can be too late if budgets are finalized.

ONE WEEK BEFORE REVIEW TIME

Prepare for your review as if it was a test in school (unless, of course, you were a procrastinator). Study previous performance appraisals, especially last year's. Study your meeting agenda and supporting documentation. Know what you've done this year and what you want to achieve next year. And by all means practice! Role-play with your spouse or friend what you want to say. Prepare a "Plan B" is case the review doesn't go as hoped, and you're not backpedaling.

ONE HOUR BEFORE REVIEW TIME

Brush your teeth. Blow your nose. Comb your hair. Straighten your tie or pull up your hose.

REVIEW TIME—THE TIME HAS COME!

Though you've submitted an agenda, the main purpose of this meeting is for your boss to appraise your performance. So, listen intently, take notes, and ask questions. As the meeting shifts to your agenda, stay calm and confident. Address the issues you want to discuss and don't be afraid to "toot your own horn." Get your supervisor to explain what measurements of good performances are to help you understand what you need to do to get ahead in your present job, move laterally, or increase your pay. Don't take offense or argue with your boss. If you disagree with something, try to find out where she is coming from and her plans for you, the department, and the company. This will help you better prepare for next year. Finally, avoid ultimatums or threats. Work together to end the review and salary outcome in a mutually positive way.

POST REVIEW

Reflect on what went well and what you would do differently next time. Compile your notes and study your goals for the new year. Create a plan to accomplish these goals and be sure to put your appraisal in a file close to your fingertips to review throughout the year.

SECTION 4
BEING A GOOD BOSS

GETTING IN TOUCH

Bill is confused. Every day on his way to his office, he stops by the message center to get yesterday's phone calls. No one will talk to him. He figures that even though he is the boss of the place, people shouldn't feel like he's an untouchable. Bill stands at the message center perplexed as people walk by him talking, laughing, and really enjoying each other. "Hi!" Bill says to every passing person. But every response is cold and lifeless.

One block up in the next corporate high-rise, Marty isn't so confused. There isn't time to be. Walking to his office, Marty is met by Paul asking him who won the company game yesterday. Then he's confronted by Mary who wants to know when he and his wife are coming over for dinner. Person after person prevents Marty, the company CEO, from getting to his office.

Get the difference between these two company leaders? One's transparent, the other has the appearance of a human brick and mortar building. One experiences life and lets the employees know it, the other barricades himself from the people in the company. One has an office, but forsakes it for the company lunch room. The other spends all day in his office rarely talking with others. We'll let you decide who's who.

Being a good leader or an exceptional boss has little to do with your experience in your field. Your employees don't care very much about your MBA or last quarter's earnings as much as they care about how you treat them. They want to know that they're loved, accepted, and understood by their boss.

It's time to start. You know you need to be more in touch with the people who are working hard all around you, but you barely know who they are.

LET'S GET STARTED

It's important that you take a moment and identify your leadership skills. When it comes to your employees, what do you excel at? We've left the lines below open for you to evaluate your ability at being a boss. Think about how others who work for you might answer the question, "What kind of boss is your boss?" When you feel you've got some ideas, write 'em down.

_____

_____

Great. We want the next few ideas to encourage you. Remember, NO ONE is perfect. If you feel you're the perfect boss, you probably aren't. But, if you feel you're the worst boss, you probably aren't that bad. Use some of these ideas for getting in touch with the people who you're in charge of in your company.

In Touch #1—Leave your office
Good things might happen in your office. The company might have done well to equip it with a super-duper computer, private fax, or maybe even your own bathroom. But all of those things actually serve to hurt your performance with your employees. So, we want you to lose your office.

That's not as bad as it sounds. Think about it. Do you know the names of everyone in your company? Do you know what they're talking about right now as you read this book? Probably not. It's essential that you leave your office every day and go where they are. You don't have to be gone long, just long enough to talk to many of them. And long enough for them to see you and for them to realize that you do care about who they are.

In Touch #2—Have them over for dinner
What do the insides of your employees' homes look like? You don't know? Do they know what the inside of your home looks like?

Want to create a strong connection with your employees? Make them dinner. Not a great cook? Ask your spouse to make them dinner. Spouse is too busy? Buy something and bring it into your home.

In Touch #3—Sharing your personal struggles
You have a personal side, right? Do the people who work in your company know

Let Them In!

It's nice to take your employees out for dinner. We're not discouraging you from doing that. However, it's vital that you invite them into your home so they can see where and how you live. Don't fall into the trap of taking them out and stopping there.

WIDE ANGLE

that? Do they know what your favorite food is? Are they aware of when your birthday is? Have you ever shared your most horrifying moment with them?

If you want to make an instant connection with the people who work for you, work on being transparent. This is tricky. You have to be careful what you share with people. It's not a good idea to share things that might get you in trouble, and it's certainly not a good idea to share something that might make its way into the company rumor mill.

In Touch #4—Creating an atmosphere of love
Do your employees get love at home? Probably. Do they have acceptance at

home? Probably. Whatever positive experiences they get at home need to continue at the office. That means that you are responsible for providing an environment that is warm, open, loving, and accepting.

Creating this might not be easy. And, if you work in a business that's deadline or bottom-line driven, making this happen might be more difficult.

Begin by loving people around you. Buy them gifts. Ask them about their weekend. Take time to drink coffee with them. If you live a life interested in others, an atmosphere of love will trickle down from your efforts.

GOOD BOSSING

Bossing people around is a very bad rule of leadership. But good bossing, or, the art of striving to be the world's best boss is always a good idea. In general there are some things every manager must remember if he's going to be good at bossing.

COMPANY PARTIES

Throwing a party is a lost art. It's okay to party over small things. And it's essential that you learn to party over major things. A party is a good thing. Plan one right now.

BIRTHDAYS

Everyone in your company was born. That's good news. But the potential bad news is. . .do you know when? Remembering

CATCH A CLUE

Birthdays

How in the world are you supposed to remember everyone's birthdays? Two ideas:

- **Ask your secretary to find out everyone's birthdays. Then, have your secretary buy boxes of cards and make her responsible for giving you a blank card on someone's birthday.**
- **If you don't have a secretary, you can find out people's birthdays from their résumés or employment applications. Then, write each person's birthday on your appointment calendar. Whatever you do,**

DON'T:
- **Type the address**
- **Just sign your name on the card**
- **Write something trite or generic on the card**

DO:
- **Write something from the heart**
- **Include a statement about how you appreciate him or her**

birthdays is an essential element of being a good boss. If you send a card, make a call, or even buy lunch, you're communicating much more than just the fact that you remembered. You're telling that person that he or she is important and valuable.

FAMILY CARE

Here's a new rule. The employees in your company have families. And, the minute a person walks through your doors for employment, his family becomes your responsibility.

Wait. Isn't that a stretch?

Not really. Think about it. There are good people who are working right now to make the company look good. They're thinking about the things you aren't. They might just be creating or developing something that'll take the company to the next level of leadership. You owe it to them to care for their families.

But how? First, look at the company's heath plan. Does it include families? Next look at your vacation time. Is it adequate? Could you give them another week of vacation this year? Do you give them the day off for their birthdays or anniversaries? Are they allowed to leave early for their kids' baseball games?

Whatever your strategy or plan, if you'll think about how your work environment affects your employees' families, you'll get employees who are concerned about how they can make your work environment great.

WHEN YOU WANT TO SAY YOU CARE...

So, you're stuck wondering how you can show your employees that they're loved and appreciated? We're giving you thirty (at no extra charge!) ideas to get you started in the wonderful world of appreciating your employees.

- A warm handshake
- Cards telling them you appreciate them
- Candy on your desk
- Free doughnuts at break times
- Stand at the elevator or entrance and give them high-fives
- Give them an extra day off once a quarter
- Smile all the time
- Ask their opinions on important company decisions
- Let them check their home E-mail at work
- Throw a once-a-year surprise birthday party
- Begin an "employee of the month" program
- Have free coffee and Cokes available through the workday
- Walk around the work area thanking everyone for their hard work
- As people are going home for the night, give them fast food restaurant coupons
- Ask your employees what you could be doing better
- Pay them what they're worth
- Promote them when they deserve it
- Provide a safe, honest work environment
- Be sensitive to any family problems they might have

- Provide them with the best work equipment you can afford
- Remember their anniversaries
- Establish a benefit plan that cares for them
- Give them movie tickets
- Create an employee break room that's comfortable
- Tell them your employment history
- Invite them to attend a sporting event with you
- Ask them to eat dinner with you and your boss
- Help them with a project at their house
- Send them an on-line greeting card
- Begin offering mid-morning breaks and encourage people to meet with those they've never met

CONDUCTING PERFORMANCE REVIEWS

It's that time of the year. You've got to evaluate the people who have given their all for your business. Sweat beads on your forehead. This is the part of being a boss that you like the least. Oh, it's fine for the people who are excelling. That's the wonderful part of evaluations. But for those who are not performing up to your expectations, evaluations are equal to getting a root canal. They're just no fun.

Whatever your feelings about performance reviews, we want to share with you some general guidelines that will enable you to be more effective as you carry out this necessary task. We'll give 'em to you in four easy steps.

Step One: Announce that reviews are coming
When you plan on doing performance evaluations, it's a good idea to tell people way ahead of time. Pop-reviews don't work well with people who work for you. So, whenever you have company meetings with your employees, announce that you'll be doing performance reviews in the next six to twelve months.

Once you've announced that you'll be doing reviews, begin making mental notes on how each employee is doing. Evaluate based on attitude, performance on the job, and their job description.

Step Two: Post a review schedule
You might not want to post it so everyone can see, but you'll still need to tell employees well in advance that their reviews are coming. This will help them prepare, and they'll know not to schedule anything on the day of their reviews.

Posting, or informing in advance that a review is coming up, is another way to prepare your workers that they're going to be evaluated. It demonstrates that you want to be an employer that deals fairly with your workers.

Step Three: Evaluate in private

If you don't have a set of ideas you're already planning on reviewing your employees by, consider the following areas:

- Evaluate based on their job descriptions: Are they fulfilling them? Based on company policies: Are they following them? Based on others' reactions: Are they easy to work with? Based on your interaction: How do you feel about them?

Things to Think about As You're Evaluating Your Employees:

- How well do they get along with their fellow workers?
- How well are they fulfilling their job descriptions?
- How are they balancing their personal lives with their work lives?
- How are they doing with their vacation and time off? Taking too much? Not enough?
- What do you hear other employees saying about this person?

- Evaluate based on places they've excelled. What are they doing really well that you want to compliment them about? Where are they outperforming their coworkers?

- Evaluate based on areas they need to grow. No one person is perfect, and this area helps your employees know that. Be sure to think through their weak areas, and make notes about how you can help them grow and get better.

- What action steps might you want to give to this employee? What goals can the two of you agree need to be met, and when might you want those ideas conquered?

Step Four: Pray

It's often said that the best way to approach things is to pray and ask God for leading and enlightenment. And, while it is said so often that it becomes almost invisible, asking God to help you evaluate the employee He's given you is essential.

Step Five: Conduct the review

- Begin by welcoming the employee to the interview. If you can, choose a non-threatening location to conduct the review.
- Begin by explaining your purpose for conducting performance reviews. Explain to your employee that you evaluate everyone because you want the company to be the best it can be.
- Ask the employee how he feels he is doing. Listen intently for areas in which he feels strong or weak.
- Begin with praises. Tell this person everything he's doing right. Be very liberal and very expressive with your feelings. Overdo it. Be sappy if you feel like it. This is your chance to affirm your worker in his strongest areas.
- Move on to the areas where performance is satisfactory but might need improvement. As you approach these areas, be firm but understanding. You might say something like, "I love what I see you doing in this area, but I think there are a few things you might not have thought of."
- Finish by assessing areas in which your employee might need to grow. These areas are ones that you feel are the weakest for your employee. Again, be firm, but understanding. Remember, no one is perfect. And your goal is to help this person be the best he can be.
- Ask if he has any questions about what you've said. Be clear and succinct in your responses.
- Set a plan for how the two of you will work on the growth areas. When you set these goals, be sure to schedule a follow-up meeting to assess growth. Make sure that you affirm that you'll help him work on these areas.

Here's a tool that you might want to reproduce when conducting employee performance reviews. Feel free to change, adapt, and re-type according to your company.

Name:_____

Date:_____

Position:_____

Position Description:

(If the employee has a written job description, it's a good idea to attach it instead of filling in this area.)

Areas I see perfect performance:

_____

_____

Areas I see good performance:

_____

_____

Areas I see need growth:

_____

_____

Goals: Things to work on before next evaluation:

_____

_____

THE RAISE FACTOR

You've completed your reviews. Now here's where it gets tough. It's time to give a little reward to your employees. You need to give a raise, but how should you go about it? Knowing when to give a raise, what appropriate behavior you want to reward, and how much to give as a raise isn't easy. A lot of giving a raise is relative and based on a number of varying factors. Consider the following ideas as you weigh raises in your business.

Based on reviews
After review time is the most normal time to give raises. And, because you've just reviewed them, it's appropriate to base raises on the reviews the employees received. Based on their reviews, you can reward them on their performances, their efforts, their accomplishments of specific growth issues you highlighted, etc. Actually, anything you saw that you liked can be the basis for a raise.

Based on performance
If you've got someone who's astounding you with their abilities midyear, or you've got an employee who's demonstrated marked improvement, it might be time to give a raise. Giving employees a raise based on their performances doesn't have to be attached to their reviews. Consider giving raises to employees who meet their goals before the agreed-upon accomplishment date. Or, why not give a raise to an employee whom you feel has done an outstanding job on a project? Remember, raises don't have to be huge. You can give small raises (or even bonuses) to employees that might

not make much difference in their financial bottom line, but might serve to encourage them to work harder.

Based on need

Millie is a great employee. You love the way she has organized the office. There's no real reason to give her a raise based on performance. But lately Millie has been letting you in on the details of her life. Her kids have made repeated trips to the doctor for the flu and various accidents around the home. Even though you have an adequate insurance policy in your company, the deductible is hammering away at her finances.

If you encounter a problem like this in your company, it might be possible for you to give a onetime bonus or small raise based on financial need. If you consider giving raises based on need, you might want to encourage receiving employees not to tell other employees what you've done.

REMEMBER THESE RAISE TIPS

Whenever or whatever you do with raises in your company, remember these important elements of every raise you give.

- **Be fair**

  Your employees will talk about the raises they got with their coworkers. So, every raise you give needs to be fair. If you base it on a particular rating system, that might not be a problem. However, if you base your raises on your feelings on performance or after reviews, it might be more difficult to be fair or explain your fairness. When you give a raise, make sure you've thought through why you're giving the raises you are, and be prepared to share that information.

- *Be realistic*

    If you've got a lot of employees in your company, you might not be able to afford a ten percent raise for everyone. Before you begin giving raises, take a look at the financial situation of your company. Then, decide how much you can afford to give.

- *Be prudent*

    It's wonderful to reward someone who's worked hard. And, if you can substantially reward her, it feels even more wonderful. However, it might not be smart to, say, give a twenty-five percent raise to someone

Who Gets the Raise?

Begin honing your raise-evaluation skills right now. Circle either "Yes" or "No" and decide which of the following employees should get a raise.

Will: He has been on time every day this quarter. In fact, he has actually been early a few times. Although he has not met his sales quotas, Will has improved his appearance.
Does Will get a raise?   YES   NO

Sheila: She used to be one of your leading employees. Reports were always impeccable. Performance was out of this world. Since her husband left, Sheila has been performing sub-par. However, she could use the raise to help cover the bills left unpaid by her absent husband.
Does Sheila get a raise?   YES   NO

Mark: He has met and beat every task you've put before him. Other supervisors are begging you to encourage Mark to transfer to their areas. Mark is an enthusiastic employee whom others say is a joy to work with. However, you and Mark don't see eye to eye on many issues. And, you've had several heated arguments.
Does Mark get a raise?   YES   NO

in your company (unless she has done something remarkable). Consider giving several small raises to someone who has done something amazing. That way you can stay realistic with your raises and give successful employees something to look forward to.

- ***Be vocal***

  It's never a good idea to give a raise, slap your employee on the back, and send him on his way. Do this and your raise-receiving employee will never know why he got more money, and he won't understand what you might be looking for next raise time. A better way is to be very vocal about why you're giving raises. Be very honest and very verbal about your reasoning for giving raises.

ISSUES OF LEADERSHIP

It's one of the hottest topics in business today. And, it's not tied to a corporate get-rich-quick scheme. It's not even about the latest health plan nor does it involve a raging new technological advantage. It's about leading a business or company so employees feel empowered, cared for, and respected.

In his book, *Aquachurch*, Len Sweet notes one essential quality that all leaders must have. Simply put, they must orient themselves by Jesus. What He did, how He lived, and even how He managed His small team of disciples is all information that we need to plug into our leadership.

So how do you do that? How can you orient yourself to The North Star without doing so in your business? And, how can you do that without imposing your specific religious beliefs on your coworkers? If you can get to know Jesus, you can do this successfully in your

Ways to get to know Jesus

- **Spend time reading about Him in the Bible.**
- **Listen to sermons on the radio or the net** from people speaking about whom Jesus is and how He lived.
- **Read current books about the life of Christ.**
- **Talk to your pastor and get his view about how Jesus lived.**

WIDE ANGLE

supervision of employees. Once you know Jesus, how He lived and how He managed people, you'll be ready to live out His love for your company and in the lives of your coworkers.

ONE MORE LEADERSHIP QUALITY...

There are a lot of leadership schemes available today. We'd like to suggest one you might not have heard of before. It's known as the "Fruit of the Spirit" leadership plan. And we're pretty pleased with it. It's based on one particular passage.

"But the fruit of the spirit is love, joy, peace, patience, kindness, goodness, faithfulness, gentleness and self-control" (Galatians 5:22–23).

Simply put, these are excellent leadership qualities to focus on exercising. If you begin orienting your leadership style according to how Jesus lived (as we mentioned above), then these fruits will begin to show up. But regardless of how you plan to lead, we'd like you to take some time right now and reflect on these leadership qualities in your life. We've placed some questions below so you can evaluate your leadership fruit right now.

Love
- Do I love the people who work for this company?
- Does my love for God reflect itself in my management of the employees?

Joy
- Am I happy? Would others say that I am a person of joy?
- Do others find joy under my leadership?

Peace
- Is our work environment peaceful?
- Am I a peaceful person to work with?

Patience
- Do I exercise patience with my employees when they're not performing up to my expectations?
- Do I hound my employees for projects when they're not in on time?

Kindness
- Am I a kind person?
- Do people feel at ease around me?

Goodness
- How well do I treat the people whom I'm in charge of in the company?
- Would others describe me as someone who is easy to work with?

Faithfulness
- Do I stick by employees who have made serious mistakes?
- Is my relationship with God evident in everything I do?

Gentleness
- Is my spirit one that attracts others to Jesus?
- Do my employees seek my advice on a variety of topics including non-work related ones?

Self-control
- Do I exercise the obligations of my job with prudence?
- Am I slow to speak when conflicts arise?

Whew! We know that was a long list, and you might need a moment to look back over that just to check what you read. Once you've taken a moment to digest what's up there, write down a few areas below that you might need to work on.

We've bombarded you with a lot of information in this chapter. Take some time right now to write some of the things you've learned about being a boss and managing your employees in the space below. After you've written your ideas, circle ones that you might try to implement in your life.

_____

_____

_____

SECTION 5
CHRISTIAN WITNESS

HAS THIS EVER HAPPENED TO YOU?

You're sitting at your desk, minding your own business. Then you catch a glimpse of a memo just placed on your desk.

You're confused. The company has never held a Sunday morning meeting. And you've promised to teach high school Sunday school this week. Since you're a Christian, you want to respond to this properly, but honestly. You feel like you're at a crossroads. You can go to Phil and explain your dilemma. But that might mean a long, possibly uncomfortable conversation about what you believe. You could just get a sub for your class. But the issue is bigger than that for you. It's not just the commitment you've made to the Sunday school, it's to your family as well.

TO: All Company Employees
FROM: Phil Wallerstein, CEO
RE: Mandatory Meeting

MEMO:
All personnel are required to attend a three-hour meeting this Sunday morning. Issues on the agenda include: health insurance policy update, raise schedule for level-three staff, and new office space reorganization.

Failure to attend this meeting will result in disciplinary action.

—Phil

So, you've got a decision to make. Write your plan of action below.

_____

_____

Now take a moment to look over your response. Think about your co-workers. How would they respond to you if you had responded this way? If you were to respond to your real boss this way, what might happen?

Being a strong witness where you work is absolutely essential. We want to take you deep into the concept of what your witness is like at your workplace. We'll examine some proper and improper ways to share and live your faith where you work.

LET'S GET STARTED!

It's best to begin on some common ground. Before we hit you with a lot of ideas, we'd like you to write down your view of what a Christian witness is and what it isn't. Getting this down on paper now will shape how you respond to the rest of this chapter. So, go ahead and write your ideas below.

What a Christian witness is:

_____

_____

What a Christian witness is not:

_____

_____

Being a witness for Jesus at work means a lot of things. Consider the implications of your presence as a believer at your workplace.

- You're a representation of God Almighty. Since God lives in you, you're His ambassador at your job.
- Christ's command to make disciples gives you a call at your workplace. Your presence as a believer where you work makes you a missionary. God has placed you strategically to be a living and speaking witness for God.
- Because you believe in God, you have some answers that others don't. The meaning of life, the origin of real love, and the creation of the

---

Got Extra Time?

Want to get a better handle on what a Christian should do or be at work? Give your responses below.

At work, a Christian must tell people what God thinks about every subject.
AGREE .... DISAGREE

When working, believers must be conscious of how God sees their fellow employees.
AGREE .... DISAGREE

Christians must dress nicer at work than coworkers.
AGREE .... DISAGREE

People who profess a belief in God shouldn't use questionable language.
AGREE .... DISAGREE

Believers have to practice a higher work ethic than non-Christians.
AGREE .... DISAGREE

world are all truths that begin with God. And you know the Truth-Giver.

• You're a lover in an unloving world. We're not saying that where you work is abusive. But even you know that the world of work doesn't always offer the affirmation that everyone needs. Because you know True Love, you have that to offer to people.

Maybe being a Christian at work isn't something you consider often. We don't want to weigh you down with guilt. And we certainly don't want you to step into a definition of being a witness that doesn't fit what God has called you to be. Let's explore one key concept Jesus made clear as He walked the earth. His words are very clear about the difference we make in the world around us.

GOOD TASTING FOOD

It can be really difficult to live your beliefs at work. And, we certainly don't want to oversimplify the task before you. But the Bible makes it very clear, and it gives solid advice about how to live out our beliefs where we work, live, and play.

"You are the salt of the earth. But if the salt loses its saltiness, how can it be made salty again? It is no longer good for anything, except to be thrown out and trampled by men. You are the light of the world. A city on a hill cannot be hidden. Neither do people light a lamp and put it under a bowl. Instead they put it on a stand, and it gives light to everyone in the house. In the same way, let your light shine before men, that they may see your good deeds and praise your Father in Heaven" (Matthew 5:13–16).

Jesus draws a line in the sand with this statement. He's saying that what we believe has to be evident in the way we live. But, is it possible to be too salty? Can you be too spiritual? Too open?

Yes.

Now, before you begin turning pages and heading for the next chapter, consider what Jesus is saying in the famous "Salt and Light" passage. Salt enhances the flavor of a casserole, but it shouldn't dominate the taste. Light illuminates a room. Too much light in a room, and it gets difficult to see. The same is true as you endeavor to live out your faith in front of the people you work with. You have got to strike a happy medium—find a way to live what you believe without making others sick: sick of us, the message, or even of God. How do you do that?

WALK LOUDLY

Loud walking goes to the heart of Jesus' message about being salt and light. What does it mean to be a loud walking Christian at work? It means that you speak very rarely about what you believe about God, the Church, and even your personal beliefs. And, it means that you focus everything you believe about those things and live the heart of those issues. The result of "walking loudly" is that people begin asking you about your beliefs based on how you're living.

- ***How can you "walk loudly" where you work?***

KEEP YOUR WORD

It's part of living out your beliefs, but it's also an attitude of being a person of integrity. What does it mean to keep your word? It means that when you say you'll be at a meeting, you're there. It means that when you say you'll have that report in, clean your desk, meet with your intern, you actually do those things. The more you keep your word, the more people will understand that you are a person who can be trusted. The more you do what you promise, you'll gain trust, respect, and integrity in their eyes.

What does it mean to keep your word? Here are some ideas:

- When you say you're going to do something, do it.
- When you promise to turn in a report, be at a meeting, meet with a coworker, it's important to fulfill that promise.
- When you agree to fulfill various parts of your job description, it's important to follow up that promise.

- *In what areas of your life are you not keeping your word? In what areas at work are you not keeping your word?*

LOVE EVERYONE

The new millennium is ushering in two very distinct relational factors. First, people are isolating themselves more. We're becoming more comfortable staying inside—surfing the net, watching the tube, or reading. Second, we're looking for people we can relate to. We're craving time away from our isolated environments and are longing to dive into real relationships with people we like and trust.

Being salt and light in the workplace offers people who are longing to take that dive someone safe to take that risk with. But in order for that to happen, we've got to love people. Christ's call urges us to treat people better than non-believing people might. If we can love them, treat them well, and be people they feel respected by, we stand in the perfect place to change their ideas about believers in the workplace.

- *How well do you treat others? Name three to five people you work with that you could treat better.*

WORK HARD

Believe it or not, right now people where you work are evaluating you based on how you work. They're looking to see how hard you work. They're critiquing your timeliness. They're scrutinizing how many trips you make to the bathroom and soda machine. They're not necessarily looking for something to catch you doing wrong, they're looking to see how you work. And, if they're aware of what you believe, they might just be looking very closely. Being salt and light in our workplaces means that we've got to be aware that people are watching how we treat our jobs. They want to know if we're thankful for having a job. They want to know if our beliefs have an impact on how we work. They're watching these things and then comparing how we work to how they work. Then, if they're impressed, or even curious, they're possibly interested in knowing more about our beliefs.

How we work is essential. It's important because everything we do serves as a demonstration of how real our beliefs are.

• **How hard are you working? Write down some areas where you could grow in your work ethic.**

GET SMART

Here's a quick test: Would you know what passages to refer to when a co-worker says any of the following?

- "Where does it say that God actually created the world?"
- "How can we know that God loves us no matter what we do?"
- "What happens if we sin and don't ask forgiveness?"
- "What does Jesus say about poor people?"
- "What does the Bible say about the end of the world?"

Okay, so maybe you don't know all the answers to those questions. And you might not necessarily *need* to have *all* the answers. But it's absolutely essential that we're prepared for the questions that others have about basic spiritual issues. And, it's important that we have proof from the Bible and even our own lives for some of those questions.

• *Do you feel you have basic answers to basic questions? If you don't, write down some issues you might want to work on.*

_____

_____

_____

BLOWING IT BIG TIME

It's not always easy to be on top of your game. It's easy to try hard to live for God at work, attempt the perfect Christian witness, and fail now and then. Ever done that? Have you ever messed up when you were trying to live your beliefs at work? Write about that time below. Then write how you handled it.

_____

_____

DECIPHERING THE MISTAKE

So, you've made a big mistake. Before you go beating yourself about the head and body, look at what you've done. Take an honest assessment of the failure. Ask yourself these questions:

- Would I consider what I did to be a major misstep?
- Was what I did a minor mistake?
- Are others talking about what happened? Or has the problem gone unnoticed?

If you've done something you consider major and people know about it, you've got more repair work to do. However, if this mistake was minor, or if people haven't noticed, then you've got more room to work. But whatever mistake you've made, it's important to be godly about making restitution with yourself, your coworkers, and most importantly with God.

• *Asking forgiveness*
The most important first step after you've made a mistake is to ask forgiveness. It's easy to let Satan lie to us and tell us that God couldn't forgive whatever we've done. However, when we make mistakes and ask forgiveness, God stands waiting to wash us clean.

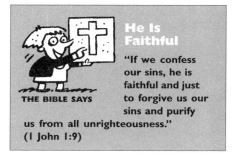

He Is Faithful

THE BIBLE SAYS "If we confess our sins, he is faithful and just to forgive us our sins and purify us from all unrighteousness." (1 John 1:9)

• *The admission*
Once you've asked God to clean you, you've got some work to do where you work. People who witnessed or are aware of your mistake might be thinking things about you. So, it's best to admit what you did to others. Be careful here. Admitting things to someone who's clueless about what you did isn't smart. If you know people who are aware of your mistake, take a moment during a lunch hour or break to tell them what happened and be willing to answer any questions. If you're honest with your coworkers, you'll be speaking volumes about your personal integrity.

• *The apology*
Your mistake might have hurt someone. You might have left a bad impression of who you are, or even who God is. And, if your actions physically or emotionally hurt another person, you've got even more serious work to do. You'll need to apologize.

When you apologize, remember to admit your wrongdoing. Be honest about what you did, say you're sorry, and ask for forgiveness.

• *The no-mess-up strategy*

Making one mistake is natural. After all, you're human. But making the same mistake again is a BIG mistake. And repeating that mistake over and over chips away at your credibility and it sheds light on a potentially deeper problem.

You might want to consider creating a strategy for not making the mistake again. Consider talking to your pastor or a close friend about what happened. Then, ask that person to help you not make the same mistake again. You might even want to commit to meeting with the person frequently to help you create and implement a strategy for not messing up again.

• *Back to your story. . .*

Now that you've read our ideas, we'd like you to imagine for a moment. You wrote your "big mess up" above. Now we'd like you to imagine that you tried one of the steps above. How might that have changed the results of your mistake?

_____

Messing up will happen. But you can control the fallout from your mistake if you're honest, open, and realize that God wants to forgive and help you stand strong for Him.

SECTION 6
CLIMBING THE CORPORATE LADDER

STRAP ON YOUR HIKING BOOTS AND CLIMB TOWARD A PROMOTION!

Living in the fast-paced job market of today means knowing what you want and setting out to achieve that goal. Part of succeeding in the workplace is becoming flexible in order to achieve that promotion which can eventually lead to working in the area you've always been interested in or saving up for that trip to Europe for your twenty-fifth wedding anniversary. While in the past, promotions required already having the corner office or twenty-five people reporting to you, the rules have changed.

Aspirations

You aspire to great things? Begin with little ones.

WIDE ANGLE

IT'S A WHOLE NEW BALL GAME FOLKS. . .

The great thing about gaining a promotion today is that the office does not have to become a rat race. There are dozens of ways to move up without the environment becoming a death match or an example of survival of the fittest.

Instead of accumulating assistants underneath you or wasting time striving for that plaque in the conference room, try taking on different jobs to gain different skills. The more experience and skills you gain will only increase your abilities and chance at being promoted. By branching out and trying your skill at different jobs, you will gain freedom and choices which lead to better projects and better groups to work with. The key thing to remember is that the people who get results get promotions. Take a look around your office or within your field. Do you see any problems? Fix them. Sense a need? Propose a new product. You are responsible for your advancement.

SIX MYTHS ABOUT PROMOTIONS

In his article, "Get Promoted without Promoting Yourself," from the June 1996 issue of *Fast Company* magazine, Bill Breen offers support for getting a promotion by referring to research done by Marian N. Ruderman of the Center for Creative Leadership in Greensboro, North Carolina. Ruderman examines the following six myths in her report, "The Realities of Management Promotions."

Myth #1: A promotion is a reward for a past performance.
Often, a promotion's context is just as important as the job's content. Some people are promoted simply because they are available (another job may have ended early and the company created another position, etc.). It is even possible that someone else has better qualifications, but they cannot make a direct move. The lesson to take away from this myth is that opportunity plays a key role in deciding who moves ahead. Knowing this, create opportunities for yourself.

Myth #2: A promotion is about matching your skills with a clearly defined position.

While it would appear that a candidate who held the most qualifications would secure the job, the reality of the situation differs. It is typically the job that is tailored to fit the candidate. Promotions fluctuate—new positions are created and existing positions are reinvented. In some cases, the position is so new that the hiring manager cannot fully define it, so he hires a qualified person and lets him or her define the job.

Myth #3: Get a five-star rating on your performance review and you will get the promotion.

Au contraire, mon frere. Just because you are doing a fab job at work does not mean that you are guaranteed a promotion. Bosses look at a lot more than your performance at work. In some cases, your supervisor may rely on his or her "gut instinct" or what others have to say about your performance.

Myth #4: Promotions are all alike—the boss finds the best person for the job.

There are many types of promotions. They range from those whose job is expanded and they get a title which acknowledges their increased responsibilities to those developmental promotions which prepare a rising star for a top position. Promotions may also be created through reorganization of the company. In this case, there may be many candidates available. Knowing this, study how your company is laid out. Discover how people are promoted in your organization and think about how to make the situations work for you.

Myth #5: Most bosses look for the same qualities when promoting people.

Yes, bosses look at work ethic, potential, and getting results. But the factor that outweighs all of these is office politics. Hiring managers are looking for people they can trust. Merit and politics play key roles. The moral of the story is notice the way that you present yourself. Your personal presentation—your communication skills and business smarts—is just as important as your work performance. It is essential to understand your personal presentation because it is who knows you that counts.

Myth #6: When you are vying for a promotion, you are competing against many other candidates.

Not exactly. The purpose of the selection process IS to choose the best person from the pool of applicants. While this is the intent, the best person is not always chosen. In many situations, the manager knows exactly whom she wants to promote, therefore only that person gets real consideration. The reasons for this occurance vary. In some cases, the individual who was promoted worked with the hiring manager in the past. Bosses will hardly be inclined to keep looking for someone if they already have someone who can do the job. Knowing the importance of visibility, try to find someone within your corporation who will mentor you. Often your mentor can put in a good word for you, giving the hiring manager an opportunity to see how great you are!

SIMPLE TIPS FOR GETTING THAT PROMOTION

1. Make sure your employer knows that you are interested in a promotion. Remember to remind your boss and the head of human resources of this often. Don't forget to make the most out of contacts. If you help someone out in another department and do a stellar job, have that person write a memo about your work to place in your file.

2. Encourage your boss to help you advance by sharing the advantages of getting someone new to take your place. ("I've loved working here, but I feel like I've really mastered the job at this point. You need someone new who is fresh and vigorous.") At the same time, encourage your boss to help you gain skills to move on to a new job.

3. Don't forget to be a team player. Being able to work as part of the team is a great asset in the workplace. Always contribute to the group.

4. When it is time for your boss to look over your work, help him or her to notice the things that

God on Our Side

"In everything he did he had great success, because the Lord was with him. With God on our side we can conquer anything!" (1 Samuel 18:14)

you have done particularly well. Don't be ashamed of doing a great job! Sometimes the office can become such a hectic place that your boss may be swamped with other projects. Help him or her to see your contributions.

5. If you want to present yourself as promotional material, make sure that you stay focused on your current job. Don't put the cart before the horse. It is too easy to become so preoccupied about getting a promotion that you lose track of the current responsibilities that you do have.

Getting a promotion seems like a pretty big deal, so big that it can overshadow other things that are important: family, friends, and your relationship with Christ. In fact, we can become so busy with climbing the corporate ladder and making a name for ourselves that we forget about why we were created and what our purpose is. First Thessalonians 2:4 says, "For we speak as messengers who have been approved by God to be entrusted with the Good News. Our purpose is to please God, not people. He is the one who examines the motives of our hearts."

Promotions have many benefits, but we must also be aware of the worldliness that can come along with them if we are not careful. Soon company lunches and working extra hours at work every week replace our fellowship with family and Christ. C. S. Lewis comments on prosperity in *The Screwtape Letters*, "Prosperity knits man to the World. He feels that he is 'finding his place in it,' while really it is finding its place in him. His increasing reputation, his widening circle of acquaintances, his sense of importance, the growing pressure of absorbing and agreeable work, build up in him a sense of really being at home in earth." If we are not too careful, we become *of* the world and not *in* it. "My prayer is not that you take them out of the world but that you protect them from the evil one" (John 17:15).

TOP 10 THINGS TO REMEMBER WHEN CLIMBING THE CORPORATE LADDER

The Business and Executive Coach at CoachU.com, Nancy Levy, has these suggestions:

1. Corporations are hierarchical and modeled after the military.
2. Line positions lead to the top, staff positions do not.
3. Learn the rules of your company's game and become a player.
4. Aim for the top.
5. Don't take everything personally.
6. Play your position.
7. Never disagree with, contradict, or belittle your boss in the presence of others.
8. An executive training program is to a corporation what West Point is to the army.

9. Don't be afraid to call a foul a foul.
10. Sing your own praises.

CATCH A CLUE

"What Are the Most Important Characteristics for Success?"

"For me it's a dedication to your real interests. It's an ability to be open-minded. Without an open-minded mind, you can never be a great success. The great artists have been open-minded, even though they may seem, like Picasso, to be very directed, you can be directed and open-minded at the same time.

"I think you have to be really intensely serious about your work, but not so serious that you can't see the lightness that may also involve your life. You have to have that lightness too. You have to not be so heavy-handed and so ostentatious. . .You might be rich, you might be famous, but you're not going to be here in ten years. That means integrity. Total integrity. A work ethic, and an ethic about work."

—Martha Stewart

DO YOU HAVE MUST-HAVE-CORNER-OFFICE-ITUS?

There is no one more annoying than Fred from accounting who got the large office at the corner of the hall with the gigantic windows and perfect view of the lake just because he discovered some bug in the system which saved the company millions of dollars. Big deal, didn't you start the hospital visitation club last year when Janet broke her hip and was in the hospital for three weeks? When you succeed at work, payoffs will come with it. While it was great that you wanted to foster a community feel to the office environment, Fred really did help the company to catch what could have been a disaster to everyone's jobs—including yours.

Envy is a tricky thing. We all know that we shouldn't covet our neighbors' new Ford Explorer, but sometimes it is just too easy. When you start envying Fred because of his new move in the office, change your attitude to one of appreciation. Congratulate Fred on his accomplishment and look to see where you can help the company improve. James 3:16 says, "For where you have envy and selfish ambition, there you find disorder and every evil practice."

PASSING THE BUCK: RESPONSIBILITY

"Holy holier than a donut, Batman!" It's Monday afternoon and your proposal for the new Mondo-Marshmallow-Milk-Chocolate candy bar is due by Friday morning (fully polished and ready for presentation to your boss). You are way behind in drafting the advertising scheme and your taste testing research data has yet to be completed. What are you going to do? Keep in mind that you know five highly-skilled individuals working in your department who could easily lend you a hand. Watcha' gonna' do? Delegate, *mon amie!*

Part of getting tasks completed in a timely and efficient manner is understanding how long a particular job should take and what skills are necessary in order to complete it. Once you've determined this, delegate certain responsibilities that will enable you to get your project finished.

1. Decide what to delegate.
2. Choose someone to complete the job.
3. Explain the purpose of the assignment.
4. Delegate the job.
5. Let 'em at it!

Once the project is underway, make sure to give them enough space to work on the project. Don't be a hovering, overprotective mother about the job. They won't appreciate it, and you could be working on something else at the same time. Do remember to be available in case they do have any questions or ideas on ways to further the development of the project.

Finally, never forget to thank them publicly when the task is completed. Encouragement is always needed.

DO'S AND DON'TS FOR DELEGATING

- Do stress the importance of the job.
- Do set deadlines and offer to meet with the people ever so often.
- Offer help when needed.
- Be understanding when people make mistakes.

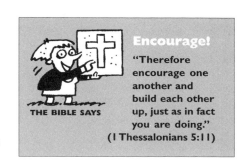

Encourage!

"Therefore encourage one another and build each other up, just as in fact you are doing."

(1 Thessalonians 5:11)

THE BIBLE SAYS

- Don't delegate something at the last minute.
- Don't be afraid to ask for assistance. The people in your office are there because they are skilled professionals who want to learn.
- Don't lose your balance in completing your tasks and delegating.

When you are being paid for your time, time is of the essence. Delegating is always an asset when you are working on a lot of things, but don't always plan on other people having space in their schedules to help you complete your projects. They too have other responsibilities! Time is important; and as they say, time *is* money. Here are a few strategies for staying on top of the work load situation.

1. Don't procrastinate.

Purchase a day-planner and use it! Prioritize and make organization part of your lifestyle. Organization is always the key.

2. *Avoid spending your life on the phone.*
Have someone screen your calls or use an answering machine. Then set aside a certain time of the day to return phone calls.

3. *Understand that it is okay to say "no."*
You cannot commit to everything.

4. *Don't spread yourself too thin.*
If you try to take on too much at once, you will only get a headache and a lecture from your boss.

Remember Ecclesiastes 3:1, "There is a time for everything, and a season for every activity under heaven."

THE HEAT IS ON...PERFORMANCE REVIEWS

Yes, the time has arrived. Ever since you began working here twelve months ago, you knew the dreaded day would arrive. And yes, it did. The almighty performance review. Janet says her's went great, that there is nothing to it. Sam, on the other hand, went to lunch and never came back. . .man!

What's the deal with these job reviews anyways? They can't be that bad, can they? Why do they cause so much anxiety? If you are feeling a little nervous as you head into your review, don't worry. Your performance is not as bad as you think.

Your Corner of the Universe

WIDE ANGLE

There's only one corner of the universe where you can be certain of improving and that's your own self.

"Most employees are doing a reasonably good job—if they weren't, they wouldn't still be at their jobs," says Mark Lifter, senior vice president of Aon Consulting's Human Resource Consulting Group in Detroit, Michigan. "Workers with performance problems know they have problems, and there's not much you can do about anxiety there."

Performance reviews are generally conducted by a supervisor every six to twelve months. Your supervisor will focus on three things: self-appraisal, improvement areas, and future goals. The more prepared you are for your evaluation, the better. Knowing this, keep a journal or record of your accomplishments at work that you can refer to during your review. As it gets closer to the time for your evaluation, talk about it with your co-workers and find out how theirs were conducted and what you can expect from your boss.

The best way to handle your review is to go in with a positive attitude. The whole purpose of this meeting with your boss is to discuss your strengths and areas where you can improve to do your job better. Don't feel like it's only a time for your boss to talk though, you get to

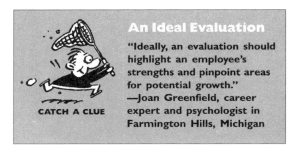

An Ideal Evaluation

"Ideally, an evaluation should highlight an employee's strengths and pinpoint areas for potential growth."
—Joan Greenfield, career expert and psychologist in Farmington Hills, Michigan

CATCH A CLUE

share too! The more you share with your supervisor regarding your performance, the better you'll perform! It's all about communication.

Performance reviews typically become a source of terror because they are handled in the wrong manner. The best way to keep your review meeting focused is to set goals. Make sure that your employer defines what he or she expects from you on the job. Bosses often forget to explain the standards that they use for evaluating a good performance. If you and your boss set goals together, your meeting won't become a downer, and you'll want to come to work the next day because you know what is required of you in order to perform well.

HOW DOES MY EVALUATION AFFECT MY INCREASE IN SALARY?

In many companies, your raise depends on your performance evaluation. But for other companies, the organization's performance is the key factor in determining raises. Whatever way your company decides to handle the issue of pay increase, your best response is to "accept whatever system is in place, make it work for you—whether you're a supervisor or an employee—and make changes to the system when necessary," says Shelley Riebel, a consultant with Armada-based Michigan Business Training and Consulting, Ltd.

If you are denied a raise or promotion, don't get upset. Instead handle the situation with a professional attitude and suggest other options to a pay increase. Just remember to approach your review with a positive attitude, keeping in mind your strengths and weaknesses. By using this approach, you'll be prepared and ready to handle any criticism that may arise during the review session.

PRIDE GOETH BEFORE DESTRUCTION, AND AN HAUGHTY SPIRIT BEFORE A FALL

So Live

"When men speak ill of thee, so live that nobody will believe them."
—Plato

DON'T FORGET

Criticism can be hard to deal with. Even if you are Susie Sunshine who never gets unnerved by anything, your manager's comments during your performance review can be damaging to your self-esteem and your pride. Part of being a Christian in the workplace means being a light to those around you. Your actions will always speak louder than your words, so it's important to not let your pride get the best of you. It is natural to be pleased with the good job you did on that last proposal. You put in a lot of hours on the project, so *of course* you deserve a pat on the back. The significant thing to understand is that you should not get so caught up in your achievements that you forget to give the glory to

God and remain humble. Wanting to be successful at work is not sinful in itself. It is when we let our pride from being successful determine our self-worth that God is replaced. By handing our achievements over to God, we are glorifying Him, for it is He who gave us the talents to produce such amazing things!

WHAT SHOULD I DO IF MY BOSS IS PREVENTING ME FROM GAINING A PROMOTION?

We all have some nightmare story to share from one time or another when our bosses pushed us to the very limits of our sanity. The best thing to do if your boss is giving you a hard time is to step back and look at the situation as if you were a non-involved third party. One key way of beginning this process is looking to see what kind of boss you have. By examining his behavior, you might begin to see why he is responding to the situation in that particular manner.

WIDE ANGLE

Jot This Down. . .

Here are a few things you wouldn't want your supervisor to write down in your file after your performance review. . .

1. He would argue with a signpost.
2. This young lady has delusions of adequacy.
3. Since my last report, this employee has reached rock bottom. . .and has started to dig.
4. I would not allow this employee to breed.
5. This employee is depriving a village somewhere of an idiot.
6. When his IQ reaches 50, he should sell.
7. Takes him 2 hours to watch 60 minutes.
8. Some drink from the fountain of knowledge. . .he only gargled.
9. If you gave him a penny for his thoughts, you'd get change.
10. The wheel is turning, but the hamster is dead.

It is also critical that you assess your feelings about where you stand with the company. If it kills you to get up every morning and drive to work at this particular organization, it may be time to hitch up the wagons and move on. If you love your company and see yourself as part of its future, then it is up to you to talk to your boss about how he or she is affecting your work and the office environment. Your supervisor may not even know that you have ambitions of moving up the ladder. In some cases, if you're working for the person who hired you, he or she may think you're still a rookie.

True Wisdom

"When pride comes, then comes disgrace, but with humility comes wisdom." (Proverbs 11:2)

You may also want to talk to someone above your boss if the situation does not improve. Be aware, though, that your supervisor's boss may not be able to help you. It is always best to deal with the problem head-on.

IMAGE ISN'T JUST ABOUT A SPRITE COMMERCIAL

While your mother raised you to believe that it is what is on the inside that counts, unfortunately once you enter the business world that notion changes. Supervisors are looking for people who can present themselves as fitting the part. If you can look the part, you can be the part. Think back to the 1994 campaign debate between Clinton, Bush, and Perot. President Bush wore the typical dark blue presidential suit and red tie. To make himself appear as if he could fit the mold of the president also, Bill Clinton also wore a dark blue suit with a tie.

Chances are you might have not even noticed it, but subconsciously you may have. By presenting himself in the traditional presidential attire, Clinton told us nonverbally that he could be the president of the United States.

Put Something On!

"Clothes make the man. Naked people have little or no influence in society."
—Mark Twain

DON'T FORGET

Your presence is not just your style of dress, it is every "visual" thing about you—how you carry yourself, your excitement about a project and how you communicate with others. When you are competing against three other people of equal skill and capabilities, the person who projects the correct style will be hired. As you walk into an office for an interview, the first three minutes are the most crucial, because the hiring manager is already making judgments about you. Your posture, body language, energy, and grooming all demonstrate what kind of person you are.

Susan Bixler and Lisa Scherrer suggest in their book, *Take Action*, that when you enter a company, it's essential that you learn how to play the "dress game." Observe how others dress in order to see how you should appropriately attire yourself. It is very difficult to climb the corporate ladder if you are not willing to present yourself in the manner that your organization approves of. By dressing professionally, you are communicating that you are confident and capable. Your dress allows others to see that you relate to them and are willing to play their game.

INDIVIDUALITY IN DRESS

Dressing for success means not only looking the part but incorporating yourself into it as well. When determining how to dress for work, keep in mind that a certain style is appropriate, but then allow yourself a little room to be free and express yourself. If you try too hard to fit the mold, you won't reflect your personality, and in the end you'll wind up feeling ill-at-ease when at work. Respect yourself and dress professionally in a manner that is fitting to you.

STAY POSITIVE

Attempting to climb the corporate ladder won't be easy. It requires a lot of work and dedication to your goals. Here are a few ways to stay positive and feel better about yourself by focusing on things other than your job:

1. Exercise more.
2. Spend time learning about an outside subject that interests you that does not conflict with your job.
3. Do volunteer work.

4. Join a support group.
5. Listen to self-help tapes.
6. Allow yourself down time to relax.
7. Hang out with people who build you up.
8. Keep a journal.

DON'T FORGET

Check It Out!

In order to help you climb even further up the ladder here are a few books to check out so you can get on your way!

- *Take Action: 18 Proven Strategies for Advancing in Today's Changing Business World* by Susan Bixler and Lisa Scherrer
- *One Minute Manager Balances Work and Life* by Kenneth H. Blanchard
- *How to Love a Job You Hate* by Jane Boucher
- *Why Climb the Corporate Ladder* by John M. Capozzi
- *Passing & Pedagogy—The Dynamics of Responsibility* by Pamela L. Caughie
- *How to Hold Your Job: Gaining Skills and Becoming Promotable in Difficult Times* by Arnold Deutsch
- *Get What You Deserve!* by Jay Levinson and Seth Godin
- *How to Be a Star at Work: 9 Breakthrough Strategies You Need to Succeed* by Robert E. Kelley
- *Moving Up: Proven Strategies for Career Success* by Edward Mrvicka
- *Embracing Your Potential: Steps to Self-Discovery, Balance, and Success in Sports, Work, and Life* by Terry Orlick
- *24 Hours to Your Next Job, Raise, or Promotion* by Robin Ryan
- *How to Negotiate a Raise or Promotion* by Donald H. Weiss
- *Academic Achievement and Job Performance: Earnings and Promotions* by David A. Wise

SECTION 7
WHEN IT JUST AIN'T COMIN' UP ALL ROSES

TAKE TWO AND CALL ME IN THE MORNING

There's a reason they call it work. It's not recreation.

Some of us may have fun at work. That is certainly the goal: to make our living at something we love doing. But the reality is that many of us are on the way but haven't arrived at that perfect match between what we love and what pays the bills.

And even if we are in the perfect job, there is not a position in this world without its own hassles and worries. At some point life conspires against us with obstacles that cause aggravation, stress, and worry. Work does that. We worry about things like

- whether our job is secure
- whether our boss is pleased
- whether our coworkers are going to make our lives harder or easier
- whether the materials will be delivered on time
- whether the work we subbed out will be adequate
- whether everyone will show up or not
- whether the equipment will work
- whether the system will crash
- whether the weather will work with us or against us

When you think about it, there are loads of unknowns that can cause stress, worry, and anxiety at work. Yet you will most likely have to continue going to work, if not to your current job, then to a new one. And if you've ever changed jobs, you've surely found that the grass may be greener on another side of the fence, but it still needs to be cut. As long as work involves humans trying to get something done, there will be some stress.

Part of dealing with work-related worry is no different than dealing with worry anywhere. It's often a matter of thought control. You simply have to stop yourself mid-worry. When your mind starts spinning out of control with the "what ifs," you have to find a way to put on the brakes. We usually think of worry as about something specific, but that specific thing is not always a *real* thing. Sometimes it is a potential thing or a possible thing. The bottom line is this, if you can do something about it, do it. If you can't do anything about it, worry is not going to make it better. In fact worry creates an aura of paranoia around you and inside of you that is distracting and diminishing. Worry stands in your way of working well. Worry drains energy that you could use on something more productive. If you are worried, your energy would be better spent identifying what you are worried about and outlining what, if anything, you can do about it.

CATCH A CLUE

Tips for Getting Perspective

Take a breath. Stress, worry, and anxiety put us immediately into reaction mode. We lose sight of the fact that we have any control of our lives. Take a breath. You do have *some* control over *something*. Find that one thing, take a breath, and tackle it.

Quiet the voices. When we are under stress, the thoughts in our heads are so rushed and so whirling that it's hard to pin any one of them down. Practice quieting the momentum of those thoughts. Thinking about twenty things at a time is going to be no more effective than thinking of one thing at a time. Just because you think about more doesn't mean you get more done. Pick one concern and see it through.

Imagine yourself two years from now sitting across the table from someone who is in the very situation that you face at work. Your current situation will be far behind you, but you are describing it to your young friend and telling them how you handled it. Think about what you would tell him and how different your anxiety level would be from what it is now. That day will come! Bank on it emotionally now.

While worry is about something specific, stress and anxiety seldom are. If worry were raindrops, then stress and anxiety would be the clouds. When we think of stress or anxiety we often think about that feeling that something is wrong or that something bad is going to happen. Often there isn't a specific scenario tied to it. It's an overall state of mind.

Stress and anxiety are bred in workplaces where we feel unsure of whether we can get the job done. When we are asked to do too much in too little time at work, we often feel stressed. When we work for a boss who is never pleased, we live in anxiety paradise. When we have to juggle jobs or minutes or employees and function on overload, anxiety and stress often pile up before we are aware and more than we expect.

The difficult thing about dealing with stress at work is getting your breath from the stress long enough to form a strategy. The very nature of a stressful job is that it asks too much of you in some way and keeps you pushed to the edge. Whether that is the emotional edge of a job with an explosive supervisor or the physical edge of a job that has too much to do, the edge is a precarious place. The first step away from the edge is to devote some time to survey the situation and make a strategy. Look for some time that you can take off work, even a day or a few hours, but time that is specifically designed to help you get your head together.

When we function under stressful situations, we become like toy trucks whose wheels are all headed in different directions. Sometimes it takes backing up to get our wheels aligned so our momentum actually gets us somewhere besides going in circles.

Ask a friend (preferably outside of work) to be a sounding board. Ask him to help you decide what about your situation can be changed or fixed and what has to be either accepted or walked away from. Let him play the devil's advocate to help you clarify what you are struggling with specifically at work. Let him role-play your difficult person so you can "let 'em have it."

After you've talked with someone to get your thoughts outside of your own head, put pen to paper. Pretend your problem is someone else's and put on paper what you think should be his strategy to make his job a better fit. Then start working that plan, adjusting and evaluating along the way.

Whether you think you can make your job a better fit or not, whether you have a plan or strategy that will work, start this moment lowering your stress at work by changing your perspective. Yes, your job is important. Also, your job is *just a job.* Your job is not your entire life. You have family and friends. (If you don't, you should be more concerned about that than you are about work.) God has given you a span of years to do something with. That something will involve supporting yourself, but if you think facing your boss is intimidating, consider this: one day you'll stand before God and give account for your life. Do you want to stand there and admit that you spent most of your adult life energy worried about work?

Whether you can make your job any different is part of the picture. Whether you can change your own attitude and make yourself different is the bulk of the picture. In the end you may leave your job, or you may change your job but, above all, make the most of your life and don't let the stress of your job cloud everything else.

HANDLING ADVERSITY

Stuff happens. Whether it's a death in the family, a child being sick, a co-worker who is impossible, or a deadline that gets moved up, adversity strikes somewhere, somehow.

The first thing you've got to figure out about your adversity (misfortune, distress, hard luck, trouble) is whether it is related to work or to home. The second thing you've got to figure out is how to keep it at one place or another. In other words, if your spouse is driving you crazy, don't take it out on your boss, and if your boss is driving you crazy, don't take it out on your spouse. (Of course you can fill in that sentence with any of the people that enter the picture.) The point still is, keep your work stuff and your home stuff as separate as possible. This is the professional thing to do, and it

DON'T FORGET

Remember. . .

The role of your company is to look out for its customers and thus its profit line. That is what your workplace is about. It's up to you to look out for yourself and your role at work. Don't be disappointed if your boss seems unsympathetic. It's not his or her role to be of personal support to you (unless you're married to the boss, and that's another set of stress all together.)

Don't be afraid to make suggestions about how you can be the best person possible at work. If it's not your employer's role to do that, who else's would it be?

will minimize the chances that you'll lose every sane or safe place you have.

For most people, both their homelife and their worklife are priorities. If families weren't important, we wouldn't have one. If jobs weren't important we wouldn't have one of those either. Unfortunately when hard times hit, we are often forced into a position of choosing between the two, and it is *never* an easy choice. If your business needs 150 percent to get the big project wrapped up, then what will you do about the soccer games you'll miss or the big event your spouse asked you to attend six months ago? If your family needs 150 percent, then how will you take time off to make it happen and still keep your work responsibilities covered? And if you've worked for any time at all, you probably already realize that often both areas of your life will need at least 150 percent at the same time. While you've gotten used to stretching yourself to a thin and haggard two hundred percent, moving it up to three hundred percent is just not going to happen without somebody paying—and you can guess who that somebody is.

Here are some suggestions to keep all the plates spinning. If a family problem is threatening to interfere with work. . .

1. When you take a job, make sure you let them know how important your family is to you and what safeguards you have in place to keep family needs from keeping you from doing an effective job.
2. When you ask for time off, ask in a professional tone. Communicate through your tone of voice and demeanor that this is a reasonable request.
3. Don't draw attention to your family trouble unless absolutely necessary.
4. Whenever you have to ask for exceptions or favors, also state how you intend to cover the time missed or return the favor.
5. Pay attention to your looks. Often family stress leaves us haggard. Simplify your clothes and your makeup (if applicable) so that you come to work with a "finished" look even though you have less time and concern for that area of your life.
6. Find a trusted friend or coworker who you can review your work priorities with a checks and balances system to make sure you are keeping the essentials covered.

7. If the crisis is going to be a long-term one, go to your supervisor with your strategies for keeping it all together.

8. If at all possible, don't spill over at work. Keep your problems at home separate. Don't become the daily check-in point for everyone to worry about.

If a work problem is threatening to interfere with home. . .

1. Talk, talk, talk to your spouse about the specifics of what is going on at work.

2. Tell your children as much as they need to know about the fact that your work is asking some extra (whether it's time or energy) from you for the time being.

3. Enlist your family to help you face this difficulty.

4. Think ahead to the coming weeks and try to get childcare or a support system in place while you are getting work back in balance.

5. If you miss significant events, find ways to be a part after the fact. Send a video camera or set aside time to hear about the event.

6. Try to be completely at home when you *are* at home. Find a way to leave work at the office even if work feels like crisis mode. There is no crisis more urgent than your kids being happy and loved.

7. Remember that work is important, but it is not everything. Urgent is not the same as important. Urgent will pass. Urgent isn't an excuse to give up what's important.

8. Don't continue to push yourself to accomplish or handle situations that, in reality, you can't. Too often we keep telling ourselves, "I'm handling it," when what we mean is, "I'm holding it in here, but dumping it there."

9. Don't fail to make choices just because they are difficult. Whether it's a confrontation or a simple "no". . .if it's necessary for your total life to be better, then do it.

CONFRONTATION

There are a few among us who thrive on confrontational kinds of communication. For most of us, though, confrontation is a tricky and uncomfortable thing. This is true both personally and professionally. In the personal realm, the feelings of significant friends and family members are at stake. In the professional realm, there is an additional level of not just people's feelings, but their jobs and yours. Because of this, when you get into a confrontation at work, whether you initiated it or not, you need to walk carefully and carry a big book about win-win negotiations.

Confrontations come in all shapes and forms. They also work in a lot of different directions. Confronting a supervisor has a whole different texture than confronting a coworker or an employee. Each can have a lot at stake, though. You'll find the same dynamic when you are on the receiving end of the confrontation. The outcome of a confrontation, no matter which direction it moves on the corporate ladder, can be just as crucial. The biggest difference is that if you are on the receiving end, you have a lot less time to prepare your response. Here are some practical points for confrontation no matter which direction it flows on the chart or whether you are on the giving or receiving end.

- **While it's often a good idea to write down your thoughts beforehand, when it comes time, it's better to say the words to the person than to write them down in a note, letter, or memo.** As difficult as it is to regret something you've said, it's worse when you (and someone else) can read and reread it over and over again. Add to

CATCH A CLUE

Before You Do Another Thing...

If you need to confront an employee you supervise:
- Think about how you would like to be treated.
- Identify in your own mind the bottom-line issue before you sit down to talk so you don't chase rabbits.
- Understand what you want to accomplish before you begin. Imagine the mood you'd like to close the conversation with or how you'd like the two of you to leave the room after talking.
- Give the employee time to think and respond.
- If you are asking for a specific action, set a deadline for a response on the employee's part.
- Be honest. If you try to sugarcoat the truth, it could make it worse, because it can feel like condescension.

If you need to confront a coworker:
- Make sure you are confronting him about something that is work-related. Don't spend time and energy on personal jealousies or petty disagreements disguising them as work issues.
- Find a time and place that won't take away from either of your work time.
- Be specific and up-front about the change you are hoping to bring about by talking with the person.
- Leave time for him to respond and be prepared that his response might send the conversation in a new direction.

If you need to confront a supervisor:
- Think through your supervisor's probable responses ahead of time, but be prepared to be surprised.
- Be realistic. Your supervisor is not going to tend toward change unless it benefits him or her. Include those benefits in your information.
- Don't do something that will threaten your job unless you are willing to walk out the door unemployed.
- Think about what kind of communication your supervisor usually responds best to. Be sure and open with that kind of communication.

that the fact that the reader reads his or her interpretation of the tone into the words, and you've got a mess in the making.

- ***Don't confront somebody when you are angry.***
 A basic, yes, and yet still we want to go to someone when we are feeling our most passionate about a subject. When that subject is an area of disagreement or a confrontation, anger is not a friend. Not only does the content often get blown out of proportion, but the intensity of the way you present the content gets blown out of proportion. In some ways it is more difficult to confront someone when you are no longer heated about what he has done, but if the issue at hand is important enough, it will be important whether you are angry or not. When you are less angry, you will concentrate more on what is at stake and be less likely to attack the person instead of the issue.

- ***Don't confront in a public place.***
 Many of us have felt the embarrassment of being confronted with other people around. Whether you are right or wrong, whether the confrontation is justified or unjustified, it becomes about something else. Rather than being a simple (or complex) issue between two people in the workplace, it becomes potential water cooler conversation. The loss of dignity becomes an issue in and of itself, and the original intent of the conversation can be lost entirely.

- ***Know what works for that person.***
 Each of us has our own preferences and idiosyncrasies. Each of us has our points of pride and our places where we can bend. If you are headed toward a confrontation, take a moment to think about the person you are about to present with difficult information (if it wasn't difficult information, it would be called a conversation rather than a confrontation). Think about how you can present that information in a way that

she will understand it and accept it, even if she isn't totally agreeable to it.

- ### *What will you really accomplish?*
  Is it worth the risk? Before you enter into a confrontation, make sure that you have tried every other way to get on the same page with someone. Whether you are confronting your boss about some way in which you've been treated unfairly or one of your employees about his behavior, start with the easiest way to communicate the information and then move up rung by rung. Particularly if you are confronting someone who has power over your position, you want to try every comfortable way of communicating your thoughts before you try an uncomfortable way.

  Confrontation has an important place. Sometimes there is no other way to come to an agreement than to hash it out. Sometimes there is no better way to be heard than to calmly get in someone's face. Always confront like you would do surgery, with great preparation and with the utmost care.

DISCRIMINATION

Discrimination on the job takes a lot of shapes. The most basic definition of discrimination is any time you are held back from a benefit or opportunity because of your race, color, national origin, gender, religion, age, disability, political beliefs, sexual orientation, or marriage and family status. In our country that kind of treatment is illegal.

If you believe that you have been discriminated against, then there are specific routes you can take to receive some kind of change. First you need to decide what kind of change you want. Were you fired because of your age rather than the quality of your work? Then what do you want to make right? Do you want your job back? Do you want to be compensated? What would be fair to you?

You also need to decide if it's worth the battle. Are you willing to go against the current and suffer the consequences? Are you willing to deal with attorneys and claims and courts? Decide before you start how far you will go to right the injustice that you feel you've received.

DISPARATE TREATMENT

There are two basic categories for discrimination. Disparate treatment is an individual case. It is when someone is treated differently because of his or her membership in a protected class, such as a minority or gender or race. Actually since gender is considered a protected class, everyone is in a protected class of some kind. The real question is, did you receive this treatment particularly because of your membership in that class?

DISPARATE IMPACT

This is the kind of discrimination that happens when the very structure of an organization discriminates against a class of people. An example: if physical requirements (not necessary to the job) for being a policeman automatically set the bar so high that women could never pass, then those requirements have a disparate impact. In this case you would have to prove that those requirements are not necessary to do the job and so they should be lowered.

While dealing with a discrimination case can be complicated and expensive, at the root the process is a simple one:

1. The employee must state that he is in a protected class and that he suffered an adverse employment action (something affected his job negatively: position, pay, title, hours, vacation. . .) directly because of his status in that protected class. For instance, "They let me go because I'm old and they could hire someone younger for less money."

2. The employer must then take a position to explain why the action happened, and he must show how it is not relevant to the employee's status in a protected class. For instance, "We were downsizing, Mr. Judge! It had nothing to do with age!"

3. The employee then tries to prove that the reason the employer gives is a pretext, a fake reason to hide the discrimination. For instance, "They weren't downsizing, because within two weeks they hired someone with a different title but my same job description."

WHEN YOUR BEST ISN'T GOOD ENOUGH

There are few things more frustrating than giving your best and it not being good enough. There can be hundreds of reasons why that happens and ninety percent of them can have nothing to do with you. Your best could not be good enough because

- your boss wanted someone else for the job and needs to get you out to get them in.
- the agenda given to you does not match the agenda that the *real* decision makers want.
- your position is on the way out no matter who's there or what they do.
- you have a new boss who doesn't like you.
- you have an old boss who doesn't like you.
- your job has changed and you haven't and possibly can't change with it.
- your boss's expectations are unrealistic.
- your boss's expectations change periodically without warning.
- because of some complications in the workplace, your best just isn't what it should be.
- because of some complications in your life outside of work, your best just isn't what it should be.

The truth about life is that our best is different at different times. If everything is right in our worlds—physically, emotionally, spiritually, and mentally—then our best is one thing. And this particular "best" is usually the bar we hold up for ourselves no matter what the situation is. But rarely is everything right in our worlds in all areas at the same time. Sometimes

"A man can do nothing better than to eat and drink and find satisfaction in his work. This too, I see, is from the hand of God, for without him, who can eat or find enjoyment?" (Ecclesiastes 2:24–25)

"What does the worker gain from his toil? I have seen the burden God has laid on men. He has made everything beautiful in its time. He has also set eternity in the hearts of men; yet they cannot fathom what God has done from beginning to end. I know that there is nothing better for men than to be happy and do good while they live. That everyone may eat and drink, and find satisfaction in all his toil—this is the gift of God." (Ecclesiastes 3:9–13)

"Then I realized that it is good and proper for a man to eat and drink, and to find satisfaction in his toilsome labor under the sun during the few days of life God has given him—for this is his lot. Moreover, when God gives any man wealth and possessions, and enables him to enjoy them, to accept his lot and be happy in his work—this is a gift of God. He seldom reflects on the days of his life, because God keeps him occupied with gladness of heart." (Ecclesiastes 5:18–20)

our bodies are sick and are pulling down every other part of us. Sometimes our hearts are sick because of a personal loss or the loss of someone close to us. Life happens, and if we were machines we could keep life from affecting our "best." But we are not machines, we are humans. We are whole beings and few of us can keep interoffice conflicts or personal sorrows from seeping into our best selves.

So when our jobs or our reputations with our bosses are on the line because our best isn't good enough, we can't always just work harder to make everything OK. If that would work, we'd already be doing it!

Here are some steps, not for saving face or for saving your job, but for figuring out what most needs to be saved.

1. Decide if the problem is that your performance is substandard.
2. If your performance is substandard, figure out why.
3. Go to your supervisor with a plan of how you can get back on track.
4. If your performance is not substandard, put down on paper in a short paragraph what you think the problem is.
5. Decide if this is something you can control or change.
6. If this problem is something you honestly cannot control or change, then decide if you can accept it or whether you need to look for another position.
7. If this problem is something that someone else can control or change, figure out a way to ask. Be careful and be reasonable. If your problem is that your boss is a cheating, lying creep, you really can't ask him to change that without losing your job, so that doesn't count as something fixable.

At the bottom of it all, it might not be *your* problem that your best is not good enough, but it is still your life to decide what to do with. It's never fun to feel like you're failing. But feeling like a failure is not the same as *being* a failure. Don't get the two confused. You can face whatever the situation is and you can work through it. Whatever the outcome, there are better days within your grasp. Just keep thinking it through—defining problems and discovering options.

WHEN YOU'VE JUST BLOWN YOUR DEADLINE

Maybe you saw it coming or maybe something went wrong at the last minute, but most of us know that "uh-oh" feeling that comes from a failed project or a missed deadline. There's a dull thud in your gut that is unmistakable.

You might have heard the expression, "It's easier to ask forgiveness than permission." Dealing with something after the fact rather than before might be to your advantage in some situations (usually husbands say this after their wives blow up at them), but in the case of the unfinished project, dealing with it as early as possible can save a lot of grief. Unless you work in a vacuum, what you do usually affects other people. If you let them know ahead of time that you are in a crunch situation, then they may be able to juggle their schedules and even find some convenience in the rescheduling. On the other hand, if you pull the plug at the last minute, they aren't only put out by you not coming through, but also, by the way you have messed with their scheduling.

Also remember that "thanks for your patience" is usually a better approach than, "I'm so sorry." You may be sorry, but don't communicate that to them. Many things can go wrong in a project. Don't assume a victim kind of position. Let them know that you are a professional *and* human, and if there was any possible way to avoid this you would have. In the meantime, to salvage both the project and their schedules and good graces, be ready with an alternate plan and let them know that everything is in the works.

Finally, be willing to pay a reasonable penalty. If you've missed a deadline and the boss comes around checking up on you on the next project, don't get defensive and fume. In fact, be proactive and ask if he or she would like a schedule of check-in points so that you can work together at keeping things on track. Always give the impression that your highest priority is getting the work done and doing the best job possible rather than defending yourself.

SECTION 8
ETHICS

WHAT'S BLACK AND WHITE AND GRAY ALL OVER? CORPORATE AMERICA

And not just Corporate America, but also America in general! Why? Because Corporate America is made up, for the most part, of Americans. We Americans have become pretty gray over the years. Our sense of right and wrong has become diluted. Situation ethics has played its role to confuse us and to entice us to believe that what's right and what's wrong can change with any given scenario.

The problem is. . .in regards to ethics, that is sometimes true. We would have no problem if each ethical decision fell plainly in the right or wrong category. We would still struggle to *do* what's right, but we wouldn't struggle to *know* what's right.

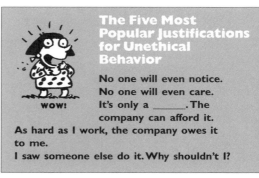

The Five Most Popular Justifications for Unethical Behavior

No one will even notice.
No one will even care.
WOW! **It's only a _____. The company can afford it.**
As hard as I work, the company owes it to me.
I saw someone else do it. Why shouldn't I?

But we often do struggle to know what is the right thing to do. Circumstances and loyalties can become so convoluted that it's difficult to know which stand you are taking and which you are standing against.

No matter whether the corporation is a large publicly-owned entity or a sole proprietorship, ethical questions are still involved because no matter how much accountability our tax forms offer us, we can all get around the truth if we want to. And if we want to, then we are facing a dilemma of our work ethics.

At theoretical levels, our current cultural climate doesn't like to spend energy on right and wrong. We have worked so hard to become more accepting of each others' differences. We have lumped "right and wrong" in the same category as "color of skin" and "gender." Yes, we should hire the best person for the job no matter their cultural background or gender. No, we shouldn't hire him if he is a liar and a cheat. It's not the same thing. A person's ethics are not a physical trait; they are a code of behavior that the person lives by whether it feels good and gets him ahead or not.

Ethics are a whole game when you move out of the theoretical and into the everyday-practical-living area. We might defend someone else's right to express his moral differences, but what about when he steals out of our desk or when he lies to get the promotion we were up for? Ethics is a whole different arena then. It is at that level where we have to stand our most firm. In other words, if we are not fair to our cubicle partner, then we aren't fair at all.

EVERYBODY'S DOING IT—STEALING?!

Is everybody really doing it? How many people do you know personally
who

- make personal, unauthorized copies at the work copier?
- take office supplies to use at home?
- make personal calls at work?
- make long distance calls from work?
- install software at home that is owned and licensed only for company
  use?
- waste time, whether it is talking, reading, or playing solitaire on the
  computer?
- lie on their expense reports, recording expenses that are not actually
  related to work?
- fake sick days?
- arrive late and leave early, taking long lunches and breaks?
- lie on time cards?

It would be convenient to believe that when you walk into the doors at
work, the definitions change. It would be easier to believe that what you
would never do outside of work (take something that isn't yours without
asking or considering paying for it) is OK within the walls of your workplace. But really, stealing is stealing no matter where you are. To steal is to
take something not meant for you.

So the real question is, "What is meant for you in your job?" Maybe in
your culture at work, making personal copies is considered a perk. Maybe

some personal days are set aside in your total package. You know what is yours and what isn't. If you don't know, then you have every right and responsibility to ask.

But there are still opportunities in most jobs, in one way or another, to take things that are not meant for you whether those things are minutes, hours, privileges, or products. It's not really an issue of getting caught or of losing your job. What is really the issue is how you stand before God every day and whether you will disregard His presence and His commands by taking what isn't yours.

SOMETHING DOESN'T LOOK RIGHT HERE

Most unethical situations are slippery in one way or another. They sneak up behind you. Often you are in the middle, maybe even a part of the action, before you fully realize what's been going on. But when that light dawns, you have to decide what to do about it.

You've probably heard the parable about the person who runs up to you on the bridge. He has a rope tied around his waist. He hands you the end of the rope and then jumps over the bridge. What are you going to do but get involved? That's how a lot of ethical people get pulled into the dirty little secrets of an unethical situation.

The kinds of situations you face can come from a lot of different directions and work at many different levels. At the most extreme, you might realize that the whole organization that you work for is based on unethical practices. Your choice there is probably to either join them or quit the team.

Most situations are not that extreme or clear cut, though. Most involve one or two people who affect your job. Whether it's a supervisor or a coworker, you are forced into

The Ethics Litmus Test

To clarify whether your ethics are being violated, ask yourself these questions:

CATCH A CLUE

- **Would I want my children to be treated this same way?**
- **What would my mom or kids or pastor say about this?**
- **How would I feel if what I'm doing was reported on the front page of the newspaper?**

finding a way to step out of the co-conspirator role without moving into the enemy role. That's a toughie.

Here are some suggestions:

- Plan a time to get together. Know what you plan on saying. In other words, don't go off half-cocked.
- Make it clear that you are not placing judgment on the other person's choices.
- Make it clear that what you are doing is standing up for what you are comfortable with and what you aren't.
- If the confrontation could cost you your job, then go into it willing to pack up and walk out.
- Don't go into the conversation angry.
- Focus on your common goals and try to find middle ground in achieving those goals.
- If nothing changes, be prepared to go to the next level of accountability (human resources, your boss's boss, etc.).
- Listen to the other side. Be open about the fact that there might be an element to the situation that you don't know about or haven't considered.

You really do have the right to stand by your own sense of right and wrong. Just because you are at work doesn't mean you lay that aside. But walk carefully.

NIP AND TUCK: EXPENSE ALLOCATION

If you have an expense account, then you have the opportunity to spend the company's money in order to do your job. How your expense account works is probably very specific to your situation, but the common denominators are:

- You are given a budget.
- You turn in receipts to charge against that budget.
- You categorize the receipts according to the budget.
- There are consequences for going over budget.

THE BOTTOM LINE

And in Church Ministry. . .

For many church staffers the crux of this issue lies in all that cash that you receive for trips and camps and retreats. Cash is a difficult thing to keep track of and way too easy to spend. The bottom line is accountability, accountability, accountability.

From time to time almost everyone robs Peter to pay Paul. It's only stealing when you don't pay Peter back. There's nothing like an envelope of cash in the desk drawer to offer an easy way to not have to stop by the cash machine. After all, you'll pay it back eventually.

The really sticky wicket is that all the money can feel the same anyway. The church pays you. You give your tithe. The church never pays enough to cover the overtime that you work. Put that all together and even if you forget to pay back petty cash, it can seem OK.

It's not. While it may be more work to keep all the accounts straight, do the work. Be honest. Honor God. Have integrity. Let Peter and Paul pay their own ways.

- There is a certain amount of honor required to keep the expenses solely for business.

Whenever there is a discussion about ethics that centers around an expense account, the issues usually focus on whether the expense was truly business related. Whether you are a self-employed person filling out a tax form or a salesman turning in receipts for meals and entertainment, there is probably a little room to hedge on some of your receipts and that little room to hedge is where the ethical dilemmas are waiting.

It seems obvious that some people can fudge on this issue and not be bothered in the least about it. They can pick up their buddy's bill (whether they paid for it or not) and include it with theirs and never lose a minute's sleep over it. But you know what the truth is? The truth is that whether or not they worry at night about their own sense of office ethics, it is still honorable to be honest. Just because you can find one hundred guys that cheat or lie on their expense report, don't use it as an excuse to lie and cheat on your own.

It's these kinds of issues that often make us feel like honoring God makes our lives more difficult. In this area, being honest and specific is often more work than lying and cheating. So doing the right thing is not always the easiest path. But you have to go back to why you are doing the right thing. Are you doing it to get the kudos? To go to heaven? To respect your relationship with God who is present in your life?

It's not that the line items on that expense report are so important to God. It's that your heart is. And your heart is what will determine what your hand writes (or punches in your computer).

INTEGRITY

To have integrity is to do what is right even if no one is looking. It is your commitment to obeying God and honoring your conscience even if you don't get caught.

We often describe people with integrity as people who "know who they are" or who "know what they are about." What those descriptions mean is that people of integrity make choices based on an inner compass that doesn't change according to circumstances or the expectations of other people. Their inner compasses are based on their own senses of morality.

The tricky thing is that people of great integrity can disagree on an ethical issue and still be people of integrity. We tend to think of ethics as "having" or "not having," as black or white. Ethics, though,

THE BIBLE SAYS

Wise Words

"The wise in heart accept commands, but a chattering fool comes to ruin. The man of integrity walks securely, but he who takes crooked paths will be found out. He who winks maliciously causes grief, and a chattering fool comes to ruin." (Proverbs 10:8–10)

"The integrity of the upright guides them, but the unfaithful are destroyed by their duplicity." (Proverbs 11:3)

by their very nature, live in the land of gray. They are often tricky, even slippery. If they weren't, then we wouldn't grapple with them like we do.

Our integrity has less to do with *whether* we disagree about ethics and more to do with *how* we disagree. It is out of a lack of integrity that we mistreat someone because they mistreat others. It is out of a lack of integrity that we talk about someone who gossips. It is out of a lack of integrity that we treat people differently according to how they treat us. Our integrity, our commitment to our own moral compasses, helps us stay true to ourselves in the midst of the ethical dilemmas we face at the office. It gives us the strength to expect "the right thing" from ourselves, our co-workers, and our supervisors.

HOW DO YOU STAND IN TERMS OF YOUR OWN INTEGRITY?

- Do you change opinions to please the people you may need politically for your career?
- Do you give in to temptation with no shame unless you are found out?
- Do you talk a talk that you seldom walk?

Integrity pours out of a strong sense of right and wrong and a commitment to be a true person. Settle your own sense of integrity and you have a compass to help you find your way through the ethical dilemmas that can plague your work life.

CONSCIENCE: RULES, REGULATIONS, AND YOU

The code of conduct at your place of business doesn't necessarily reflect your own conscience, your own sense of right and wrong. It doesn't have to. You are a part of a community there. The code of ethics isn't necessarily an unabridged moral dictionary of every right and wrong. It is the essentials for working together in a way in which everyone does this job in the most productive way possible. Each organization will have its own specific way of doing things and the specifics will flow out of the goals and mission of that organization.

So when you look at the rules and regs, the important question is not whether you particularly agree with each individual one. The real question is whether you are truly being a part of that community. Yes, the rule about no coffee in the conference rooms is incon-

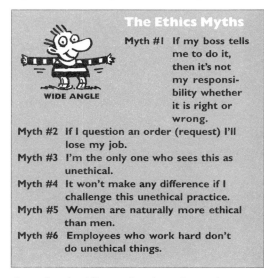

The Ethics Myths

WIDE ANGLE

Myth #1 If my boss tells me to do it, then it's not my responsibility whether it is right or wrong.

Myth #2 If I question an order (request) I'll lose my job.

Myth #3 I'm the only one who sees this as unethical.

Myth #4 It won't make any difference if I challenge this unethical practice.

Myth #5 Women are naturally more ethical than men.

Myth #6 Employees who work hard don't do unethical things.

venient. Yes, you know it was written for the idiots who don't know how to use a coffee maker and they ruin it for the rest of the group. Yes, you know how to use a coffee maker and how to keep spills to a minimum. No, that doesn't make you an exception to the rule.

Nevertheless, that rule is a part of the system that keeps peace. It is an imperfect system, no doubt, and one that will change along the way. But you are a part of that organization and one of the best ways to help the organization is to work within the rules and regulations that are established there. Some of those guidelines probably suit you well. If you disregard the ones you don't like, then how can you judge the person who disregards the ones you value? That is the essence of chaos, or anarchy.

On the other hand, when you support the system, even while establishing forums to change it, then you support the organization as a whole.

Part of being a professional is being a positive force of energy in your position. When you lower yourself to gripe about petty rules or to disregard them, then you lessen what you could be accomplishing there. The total picture of what you bring to your employer is lessened and the work you could be doing is disabled.

On all counts. . .think again.

TEMPTATION

You don't have to look far to find temptation. It is usually quite a pro at finding you. You have to remember a few things about temptation, though.

Being tempted to do something is not the same as doing it.
Almost everyone is tempted to take advantage of an opportunity in a way that is less than ethical. The fact that you might consider the opportunity only makes you human. You are not doing something unethical until you take the opening and make the choice.

The longer you entertain temptation, it is more likely that you'll give in to it.
Sometimes it just takes the time to build up the nerve to admit to ourselves that we are going to do something we are *not* proud of. If we continue to entertain a temptation, then we are not really saying "no." If we aren't really saying "no," then we're probably saying, "eventually yes." Don't deceive yourself. It doesn't take long to say no and walk away. If you're not walking away, then what are you really saying?

Saying "no" to temptation sometimes requires a change in your role or the structure of your job.
Are you tempted to be over-involved with a coworker? Maybe you should bring someone else in on the project you two have been working on. Are you tempted to "share" the supplies you purchased for the company? Maybe you need to change the system so there is more accountability for everyone, including you. Sometimes temptation lies in the very way our

jobs are laid out. Sometimes changing that structure can make temptation disappear completely.

Often, the things you are tempted to do reveal something about yourself or your life.

We are often tempted because we are missing something in our lives. When we don't get that "thing" in the appropriate places, we look for it in the inappropriate ones. Maybe you are tempted to flirt with that coworker because you are fighting with your spouse. Maybe you are tempted by petty cash because you don't have enough control over the money at home. Take the opportunity when you are tempted to look at your life and to see what

Here's What God Says About Temptation...

"No temptation has seized you except what is common to man. And God is faithful; he will not let you be tempted beyond what you can bear. But when you are tempted, he will also provide a way out so that you can stand up under it." (1 Corinthians 10:13)

"Because he himself suffered when he was tempted, he is able to help those who are being tempted." (Hebrews 2:18)

"For we do not have a high priest who is unable to sympathize with our weaknesses, but we have one who has been tempted in every way, just as we are—yet was without sin." (Hebrews 4:15)

"When tempted, no one should say, 'God is tempting me.' For God cannot be tempted by evil, nor does he tempt anyone; but each one is tempted when, by his own evil desire, he is dragged away and enticed." (James 1:13–14)

you are missing. There might be a wonderful way to give that to yourself. You might miss that if you merely give in to temptation.

You are not the only one tempted.

Yes, people struggle with different things and yes, some people don't struggle with whatever your stone in the road is. But everyone is tempted by something, somewhere, at some time. When we come to believe we are the only one who is struggling, we feel isolated, which leaves us less able to stand up to ourselves and to those forces that whisper to us in the dark.

One thing is for sure, if sin wasn't enticing we wouldn't fall prey to it. The whole point of ethics is not just the ability to *tell* right *from* wrong, but to *choose* right *over* wrong. Temptation plays its role in that choice because it forces our hand. It pushes us to say "yes" or "no" and it takes a "maybe" with complete optimism.

SECTION 9
FINANCIAL

CONTENTMENT

The question of "enough" is really a question of contentment. With how much can you be content? If the answer to that is a concrete one—a house with a bedroom for each child and enough money for two fun vacations a year—then good for you, go for it. But if your answer is an open-ended one—more than the previous year, more than my brother makes, more than anybody else I know has—then you better buckle in for a long ride, because trying to get "more" will be a lifelong pursuit.

Read the rest of what Solomon says about "enough" and contentment:

> *Then I realized that it is good and proper for a man to eat and drink, and to find satisfaction in his toilsome labor under the sun during the few days of life God has given him—for this is his lot. Moreover, when God gives any man wealth and possessions, and enables him to enjoy them, to accept his lot and*

Contentment

THE BIBLE SAYS

This is how Paul described his perspective on contentment: "I am not saying this because I am in need, for I have learned to be content whatever the circumstances. I know what it is to be in need, and I know what it is to have plenty. I have learned the secret of being content in any and every situation, whether well fed or hungry, whether living in plenty or in want. I can do everything through him who gives me strength." **(Philippians 4:11-13)** _be happy in his work—this is a gift of God. He seldom reflects on the days of his life, because God keeps him occupied with gladness of heart._

I have seen another evil under the sun, and it weighs heavily on men: God gives a man wealth, possessions and honor, so that he lacks nothing his heart desires, but God does not enable him to enjoy them, and a stranger enjoys them instead. This is meaningless, a grievous evil.

A man may have a hundred children and live many years; yet no matter how long he lives, if he cannot enjoy his prosperity and does not receive proper burial, I say that a stillborn child is better off than he. It comes without meaning, it departs in darkness, and in darkness its name is shrouded. Though it never saw the sun or knew anything, it has more rest than does that man— even if he lives a thousand years twice over but fails to enjoy his prosperity. Do not all go to the same place? (Ecclesiastes 5:17–6:6)

For many the answers are ringing in your heads before you can even finish reading that passage. _Enjoy my prosperity? When I'm prosperous_ then _I'll enjoy my prosperity! Why worry about it until then?_

Like most things in life, prosperity is a relative term. If you have enough money to have a house and furniture, by the general standards of our world economics you are prosperous. If you have food enough to eat (whether it's what you _really_ wanted or not) then you are prosperous. What keeps you from enjoying that prosperity? Thinking you should have more, right? Thinking it's not really enough, right?

The question of "enough" is an inside question rather than an outside question. It's a question of your attitude toward your wealth (money and belongings). It's not about "enough" in terms of what's laying (standing, hanging, sitting) around you, as much as it's about "enough" in terms of what is important inside of you. It's OK to have goals. It's OK to want more than you have, but don't expect to enjoy that stage if you haven't learned to enjoy the stage you are in now. Once you get there you will have new goals in mind and different things that you wish you had.

On the other hand, if you learn to be content, not only will you still have your goals and ambitions, you'll enjoy them. It's all going to be gone when you leave this world anyway, would you rather struggle through life or smile through it?

One of the reasons we don't find contentment with the way our lives are right now is this: when we decide what kind of lifestyle we want to work toward, we don't think long enough about God's call on our lives. If you don't first define what kind of life you think God has called you to, then you have no guidelines for deciding how much is enough.

Be Content!

Keep your lives free from the love of money and be content with what you have, because God has said, "Never will I leave you; never will I forsake you." (Hebrews 13:5)

The first step to contentment is not "getting enough." That's the last step, if it's a step at all. The first step is getting in tune with what God wants out of your life. Proverbs 19:23 says, "The fear of the Lord leads to life: then one rests content, untouched by trouble." Contentment comes when we have our priorities in order and our mission in life clarified. When we get those things in order, *then* we are in a position to say, "OK, the most important things are in their slots, what kind of optional stuff do I want to add in?"

Is that to say you should never ask for a raise or move to a better paying job? *Absolutely not!* Is it to say you should never have a swimming pool or a vacation home? *No, no, no.* But it *is* to say that being content right now where you are is the best place to be to decide your strategy for where you want to move next.

TITHING

If you want a good example of someone who understood tithing, take a look at the widow Jesus saw at church. If you grew up going to Sunday school, you probably heard a story called something like "The Widow's Mite." Basically the woman stood in line at the church offering boxes between the rich and well-off and offered her two small coins. Jesus and His disciples were in the room, and Jesus pointed out the woman to his followers. He told them that this poor woman really knew what giving to God, tithing, was all about. He told them that, in reality, she had given the most of all because she had sacrificed the most to give.

The disciples must have been amazed that Jesus could say that this woman gave the most of all. They could see the riches being thrown in the offering. Maybe, though, they "got it" that God receives our offering by looking at our hearts and the joy we feel in giving back to Him. By observing this woman, maybe we can "get it" too.

When we know what this woman knew, then we give in a way that pleases God.

- **She knew that giving her money to church was an important thing. It mattered.**

  The Bible teaches that we are to give of our resources to the ministries of the church. In the Old Testament the guidelines for giving were very specific. Church members gave a tenth of their money and crops. They gave their finest cattle and sheep. The teachings in the New Testament actually raise the bar in terms of tithing. The New Testament doesn't teach us a minimum that we can give and then do what we want with the rest. The New Testament goes even further than that and teaches us to give as people who feel the responsibility to minister to the world through the church.

• ***She knew that she needed to give her money even when it wasn't convenient.***
When would it ever have been convenient for a widow to give money during Bible times? Women were considered unemployable as it was. Then once a woman lost her husband, she was considered destitute, a charity case. For a widow to give at all would have been a sacrifice. Even today, though, sacrificial giving is not a luxury we afford God. It is the least we can do. We emulate God's sacrifice when we give (even if, and maybe especially if, it hurts a little) so that God's work continues in our world.

CATCH A CLUE

Here's One Way to Look at It

Malachi was a prophet who called God's people back to true commitment.
In his prophecy (the last book of the Old Testament), he says that God asks this question of the nation of Israel:
" 'Will a man rob God? Yet you rob me.' But you ask, 'How do we rob you?'
'In tithes and offerings. You are under a curse—the whole nation of you—because you are robbing me. Bring the whole tithe into the storehouse, that there may be food in my house. Test me in this,' says the Lord Almighty, 'and see if I will not throw open the floodgates of heaven and pour out so much blessing that you will not have room enough for it.' " (Malachi 3:8–10)
Malachi gives us two mind-blowing concepts to think about: (1) that we are robbing from God when we don't tithe, and (2) that when we don't tithe, we don't see God's blessing as fully as we could be seeing it.
Makes you want to run right out and find somebody with an offering plate, doesn't it?

- ***She knew that her gift mattered to God even if it was small.***
  God sees what we do even when we do it in absolute secrecy. Jesus made that clear in the Sermon on the Mount. God sees more than even the tax man or Uncle Sam does. God sees the nickels and dimes, the cash given when a check might have been more obvious. God sees our efforts and our sacrifices, no matter how small our gifts might seem in comparison to those of other people around us.

  The bottom line for tithing is this: We stop seeing our paycheck as ours and see it as God's. He gave us the job. He gave us the bodies to do the job. He gave us the minds to think to find the opportunities to do the job. We fool ourselves if we think that what we make in terms of salary belongs to us. *We* are God's. So when we give, when we tithe, we are not graciously giving God a tip. We are giving God what is already His. As for what we keep? We are merely managing His estate for Him.

  That kind of perspective puts a whole new light on what we like to call discretionary spending, doesn't it? Consider carefully what part of your paycheck God wants you to use to support the church, His body in this world. Then consider carefully how God wants you to live your life and distribute the rest of your money. No one can answer that question for you. While ten percent might be the number, pray about it so you will know if that is enough.

SAVING

The first big myth about saving: I don't make enough money to save any. The second big myth about saving: I'll save later.

There's really no formula for saving money. There is one word that is really important though: now. Start saving now.

Most financial gurus suggest that you save ten percent of each paycheck. By saving a percentage rather than a fixed amount, you will naturally increase your savings with your cost of living. By taking it out as you deposit your paycheck, you will miss it less. By taking it out of each paycheck, you miss smaller bits.

This is the big façade of savings. A little bit just looks like a little bit, but it's really not. It's really a part of a much bigger bit. When you're sitting there with the little bit, you think, *What difference will this make? I can use this little bit for something I need right now. Savings is so long-term. Savings won't miss my little bit.*

THE BOTTOM LINE

Pinch Those Pennies

A penny saved, a penny earned.
A hundred spent, a dollar burned.
A thousand spent, perhaps a meal.
Ten thousand, hope you found a steal.
Whatever's spent, it's gone for good
and won't be 'round the neighborhood.
A penny saved, a penny earned.
A penny saved, a lesson learned.

There's your mistake right there. What will actually happen is that you will spend your little bit on something short-term, and it will be gone, vanished. But, consider the alternative. If you let that little bit stay in incubation, it will grow and grow and become its own entity, an entity that you will not recognize as its little-bit former self. An entity that won't take over the world, but will be at your beck and call when you really need it.

Don't let the savings façade confuse you. Keep making the sacrifice of that little bit. Think of it as paying yourself. Most of your money will go to someone else: the utilities companies, the furniture company, the credit card company. The money you save is really the only money you pay yourself. Treat yourself well. Make yourself a priority.

If you are an employee, many companies have programs in which they will deduct savings from your paycheck before you receive it. Now *that's* the best way to beat the savings façade. If you never even see the money you've saved, it doesn't hurt as much to not spend it.

RETIREMENT

No matter how old you are, if you are old enough to get a paycheck, then you are old enough to at least be aware of what you can be doing now to prepare for your retirement. Companies are getting better and better at helping you do that. Whatever benefit your company offers, take it. Don't skip over that benefit in order to get more money in your pocket now. Retirement, in the end, is like every other area or life. Whether you're talking about your health, your business, or your kid's education. . .you can't just leave it up to the professionals anymore. You need to be hands-on if you want to make sure you are taken care of. And you need to start now, wherever you work, to get it all taken care of.

Many companies provide a plan in which you invest part of your paycheck (before taxes are applied) toward your retirement. Some companies then match or add to the money that you set aside up to a certain amount (often around five percent or your total salary). The great thing about these kinds of plans (401Ks or SEPs) is that the money is taken out *before taxes*. That is called "tax deferred." You will not pay taxes on that money until you take it out of the account (which hopefully will be after you retire). By that time, you will have earned interest not only on the money you saved from your check, but also on the taxes you would have had to pay on that money. (This is a good thing.) There is most often a limit on how much money you can invest in your 401K or a similar program. Usually that limit is defined by a percentage of your salary or a maximum set by government regulation.

You can often borrow from your own 401K. If you do, you are charged a percentage of interest that is often a larger percentage than what you are currently earning, but you are paying the percentage to yourself, so it doesn't hurt as much. Remember, though, that if you resign from the company, your loan to yourself is usually due in full. (You always have to count the cost when you borrow money—even from yourself.)

The 401(k) type plans were the first and are the most popular, but there are other plans that have similar functions.

- SEPs (Simplified Employee Pension often used by small companies, sole proprietors or the self-employed)
- 403(b)s (often used by non-profit organizations)
- 457 plans (often used by government agencies)

All these plans differ in their terms and conditions, but their basic premise is the same: take money out before taxes (tax-deferred) and let it start growing toward your retirement. Eventually you'll pay taxes, but not until your money has worked for you just as hard as it possibly can.

Something to Consider

CATCH A CLUE

If you are considering retiring early, don't just look at what you will get in your pension, also project out what you would have gotten if you'd stayed. Sometimes staying on just a few more years will make a big difference in the amount of money you will receive in your pension. Know that difference before you decide when to retire.

Some companies also offer a pension plan. This can work differently for every corporation and usually there is not a lot of customizing that you can do. The rules are already set when you're hired and usually included in whatever employee packet you receive when you start work. (Sometimes it is the pages in the back that look cumbersome and so you skip over them. Don't overlook these documents.)

A basic pension plan scenario would work this way. When you retire, your pension is doled out to you according to a formula. That formula will figure in your years of service, your average salary, and a percentage. Your company, using their version of "the formula," will figure your retirement benefit and begin distributing it to you when you retire. Often you have to be at the company a certain amount of time before you are fully eligible for this program (fully "vested"). Also, remember that pension plans often don't give you as large a benefit as a 401K or investing the money yourself, so if you have an option, consider it carefully.

Pension plans are becoming less popular with the advent of plans like the 401K but they are still around, and you might just be on your way to being vested in one.

BRINGING HOME THE BACON

One of the first rules regarding salary is to get the bases covered when you enter the job so that you don't have to backtrack once you are employed. But that's a tricky one. Certainly you should know what you are going to make and what kind of increases your company gives (merit, cost of living, etc.). But the truth in the interview process is that money is the last thing discussed, and it's usually discussed after you've committed yourself to the job, at least in your own mind. The other truth is that things often change once you get into the job. Management changes. Bosses come and go. And even if your boss is the same person, bosses go through changes that sometimes leave you feeling like you are working for a different person altogether.

So when it's all said and done, yes, you need to cover salaries, promotions, and salary increases during the interview process, but you'll also need to approach those topics after you're on the job. Here are some tips to remember.

1. Keep the big picture in mind.

As an employee, it's so important to remember that you are a piece of a big puzzle. One of the best ways to get anything done is to figure out what your team members and particularly your boss is trying to accomplish and make your plan part of the big picture. This is true in regards to strategy decisions, but also true in regards to increases and promotions. If what you are asking for doesn't benefit the boss in some way, either in what you can accomplish or in the fact that you're willing to stay, then chances are less that you'll get what you're asking for. If you can frame your request within your boss's overall plan, then you have a lot better chance of getting what you are asking for.

2. Create some opportunities for discussion that do not require immediate response but let your supervisor know what you are thinking about.

If you can have some informal dialogue before you are actually asking for action from your boss, then he or she can stay relaxed in the conversation. Be careful, though. Don't let every discussion be about what the company needs to do for you. If money is coming up all the time, create opportunities to have conversations with your boss that aren't about money.

3. Be prepared with a specific plan.

If the question gets turned back on you, be able to articulate what you want. Sure you want to make more money, but how much? Why *that* figure? How does your plan make sense in light of your duties and the pay that your peers receive?

4. Understand the channels.

Most businesses (except the small, informal, family-owned ones) have forums for discussing promotions and increases. These forums usually take the shape of periodic reviews. If that is how your company works, then make the most of that forum. Don't hold back during your review then harp on issues later.

5. Know the "whys."

Whether you think your boss will agree with you or not, know why you think your requests are fair and appropriate. Asking for more money just because you want more is human, but it doesn't work as strongly as a request with a well-thought-out rationale.

APPROPRIATE BENEFITS

You've probably heard the phrase "total package" by now. That means, not just your paycheck (or salary) but the monetary equivalent of all the benefits you receive because you are an employee of your company. Another way to look at it is your whole cost to the company.

When your company hired you, it made an investment in salary that included 7.5 percent of taxes that you would be paying if you were self-employed. They also may be paying for insurance and retirement plans. Most employers also measure days off, even holidays, in terms of monetary value. They reason that often they have to hire a sub and at the very least you get paid for work they don't receive on that day. Employers look at what you cost them, not just what you take home each paycheck. So when you decide if you are being gipped or not, remember to look at it from the company's point of view.

On the other hand, part of being an employee is the fringe benefits. If there were no benefits to being an employee, then everyone would be self-employed (what a world that would be). When you are interviewing for a job, it is fair to expect a benefits package. It is expected that this package is one of the things that enables your company to compete for the best workers.

Benefits in today's workplace can be varied and flexible. Often the list can include:

- Retirement plans
- Scheduled bonuses

- Stock options
- Profit sharing incentives
- Medical and life insurance
- Guaranteed cost of living increases
- Sick days/Well days
- Holidays
- Vacation
- Incentives for long-term commitment
- A bonus system
- Relocation and housing services
- Flexible hours
- Job-sharing
- Work hours at home
- Daycare support and services

WIDE ANGLE

Remember...

There is often more flexibility for an employer in regards to benefits than to salary. If you want the job but they can't quite meet your demands in terms of salary, maybe you can even it out with increased flexibility or time off. Benefits are often negotiable. It never hurts to ask.

- Opportunities to change or customize benefits as you go

There are a variety of ways that an employee can benefit from working for a company. Barter and bargain going into a job to get a benefits package that you can be happy with for a long time. If you fail to do that, find the appropriate channels to discuss benefits (often through human resources rather than your supervisor).

SECTION 10
OFFICE ODDITIES

FUN LUNCH BREAKS

Your lunch hour is a great opportunity to take a break from work and get rejuvenated for the second half of the day. But you don't have to spend all your time eating lunch. Take advantage of that hour and make the most of every minute. If you're tired of the whole "turkey sandwich in the lunchroom" routine and are ready to expand your lunching horizons, then look no further. We've put some fresh ideas together that will add variety to your lunch hour and help you accomplish tasks that otherwise need to be done when you're ready to call it a day. You might be surprised that you can fit more into an hour than you thought.

1. Exercise.
If your company houses a fitness center, you don't even have to get in the car. If not, look into any nearby fitness centers, health clubs, park districts, or colleges where you could work out or even play a game of basketball. Even if you have a fifteen-minute drive there and back, that's enough time for a twenty-minute workout and a quick change too. No showers nearby? Go walking. It's a great way to clear your mind and get in shape.

2. Meet a friend.
Let's face it. Outside of work, our lives are so busy. The lunch hour is a perfect time to meet a friend you don't have time to see or talk to otherwise. Share a meal, or better yet—take a walk together!

3. Try a new restaurant.
Are your tastebuds in a rut? Decide that once a week you'll eat at a new

restaurant. Scope out the yellow pages and talk to others who frequently eat out and know what's good. But don't just stick to places you know you'll probably like. Be daring and give that new restaurant you know nothing about a try.

4. Read.

It seems like there's never enough time to read a book or even a magazine, so find a quiet spot to relax and read a bit.

5. Do your devotions.

Having trouble getting up before work to read your Bible and pray? Lunchtime is your next best time to find a little quiet time with God. Try to find a peaceful spot away from your desk so you're not worrying about incoming calls or that to-do list.

6. Picnic in the park.

Enjoy the fresh air and surrounding nature.

7. Go to the zoo or a museum.

We're not implying that you spend the afternoon there. But forty-five minutes in this environment will help take your mind off work and put you in a better mood.

8. Write letters or E-mail friends.

Lunch is the perfect time to keep up with your correspondence.

9. Take your child to lunch.

If your child is in school or in daycare, try to coordinate your lunch hours. Note: Be sensitive to how your child in daycare might react. Some might find it hard to say good-bye again.

10. Visit your grandparents or someone in a nursing home.
Don't know anyone in this age group? Contact a local nursing home and get paired up with someone.

11. Get your hair cut.
And then see if anyone notices!

12. If you live close by, entertain.
It's a great way to open your home and show some hospitality. To minimize stress, get prepared beforehand.

13. Go shopping.
To all you shop-a-holics, what more can we say! Get out and make every minute count!

14. Run errands.
Do your banking, stop at the drycleaners, pick up items at the store, etc. While that doesn't sound like great fun, you'll be relieved to have these tasks out of the way so you're able to go straight home when work is over.

15. Make the most of your surroundings.
Take a look around your place of employment and get creative.

Get Away
Assess your job and your personality. If you work in close contact with people all day and need some time to be by yourself, use your lunch break to get away by yourself. Or if you're in an office or cubicle and long for some conversation, ask friends or coworkers to join you. Whatever you do, try not to eat lunch at your desk. While it may be tempting to finish one more project, studies have proven that people who get away from their desks during lunch are actually more productive than those who work straight through their breaks.

BREAKING THE CODE: FROM THREE-PIECE SUITS TO CASUAL FRIDAY

Men's lives are so simple when deciding what to wear to work. You wear a suit, tie, shirt, and shoes, and that's it. Well, hopefully socks too, but there's not much thinking involved.

Women, on the other hand, can sometimes sneak in a dressy dress and accessorize, but your business formal wardrobe is usually simple to coordinate, even on a sleepy morning. However, those days might soon be history if you

Hot Tip:

It's better to err on dressing up than dressing down.

DON'T FORGET

received the memo stating your company is changing its dress code from a business formal to business casual. Now what are you going to do with all those suits?! And what in the world does business casual mean exactly? Hopefully, your company provided some guidelines in what to wear, but don't panic if you're feeling out of touch with the fashion world. Your wardrobe consultants are here.

WHAT TO WEAR

To shed some light on business casual, we'll try to show you what it is not.

For instance, whatever you wear on Saturday morning while you're reading the paper and drinking coffee is not a good idea to wear to work. Nor would we recommend any athletic wear. Clothes that are suitable for going to a picnic, running out to the store, or just relaxing at home should be worn at those times and not to work. Remember the key phrase is "professional but relaxed." That doesn't mean trying to pass off your pajama bottoms and slippers as the new trend in fashion! You

WOW!

Casual Day Faux Pas:

1. Wearing your favorite concert T-shirt underneath a sportcoat.
2. Pretending your workout tights are nice stretch pants.
3. Wearing ripped jeans and a halter top.
4. Dressing up your black pleated tennis skirt with pantyhose and nice flats.
5. Wearing dark socks and white tennis shoes.

should still look respectable, especially if you meet with clients or have customers who visit your place of employment. A good rule of thumb is that if you question whether something is too casual, it probably is. Select something else, and inquire first.

BASIC WEAR

Still a bit confused about business casual? We've provided a list of options for both men and women to hopefully widen your casual horizons. While these items are not inclusive, they can provide a reference point for the basic casual wear.

Women:

Sweater sets, blazers, skirts, pants, blouses, jumpers, and lower heels or "flats."

Men:

Vests, sportcoat or no coat at all, long or short sleeve shirts with collars, tie or no tie, and slacks.

Be sure to have some basic pieces that coordinate with other items. For instance a black skirt, white shirt, sweater, and dark pants that can be worn with more than one thing and accessorized. Remember a scarf or different shirt can change the look of an outfit.

SHOPPING 101

When you look in your closet and feel like all you have to wear is jeans and tennis shoes or suits, it might be time to invest in some new business casual clothes. But be careful. You could invest a fortune really fast by going out and buying new clothes to fit the code. So what should you do?

CATCH A CLUE

Mirror, Mirror on the Wall

Above all else, we highly recommend looking at yourself in the mirror before leaving for work, no matter how late you may be. Consider this gal's true story:

"In rushing to get ready, I put on a sweater and then sped out the door, not realizing one of my bras had gotten caught on the back of my sweater! Needless to say, I went several shades of red when the client at my *second* sales call pointed it out. I'm not sure what the client at my first sales call thought?!"

- ***Look in your closet***
  Look for clothes that you might wear to church or when you go out for the evening that would be acceptable work attire.

- ***Shop sales***
  Most stores have sales near the middle and ends of the seasons, while some even have them at the ends of the months.

- ***Comparison shop***
  While this takes time and energy, be a savvy shopper. Most stores carry similar products but list them at drastically different prices. Take the time to look around, and you'll find some deals.

WIDE ANGLE

I'm Glad You Did. . .

"I've never had any sense of fashion, and rely on a personal shopper to help me coordinate ties and shirts. Now she helps me with my casual wardrobe and gives me tips on what looks good with what. I'd still be wearing bell bottoms if it weren't for her!"
—**Bob, Boston, Massachusetts**

- ***Outlet shop***
  While outlets often have price cuts on name brand items, do your homework in advance. Shop regular stores first so you know how much things are before buying. Why? Because many outlets offer lesser quality name brands at the same or only slightly cheaper prices. Others might show a price cut on the tag, but there's really no difference from the regular store.

- ***Catalog shop***
  There are several catalog companies that offer casual business clothes. Check out Land's End, Eddie Bauer, Chadwicks, etc.

- **Internet shop**

    If you don't get any catalogs and aren't sure where to start, check out the Internet. You don't even have to get dressed to shop!

- **Personal shopper**

    If you still feel like your fashion sense needs a little tweaking, consider a personal shopper. Usually found at the bigger department stores, he or she

Remember:

Don't sell or give away your suits just because your company went casual. Business casual is a fashion trend. There could be a move back to business formal in the future.

DON'T FORGET

will ask you questions about your likes and needs and then help you choose the appropriate clothes. A personal shopper will also look for specific pieces and call you about sales. And best of all—their services are usually free!

CASUAL FRIDAY

If your company allows even more casual attire on Fridays, you might be able to wear jeans, but be sure what you wear with the jeans is nice. Keep in mind the theme is relaxed, not sloppy. We'd hate to have you show up wearing a baseball cap and sweatpants and then be sent home after trying to explain that this book said that was acceptable casual wear. How you dress presents a picture about yourself and your company. So rather than trying to get away with being as casual as possible, take pride in your appearance.

In Focus

What you wear and how you look can quickly become a source of worry, discontentment, envy, or pride. Be careful that you don't focus too much time and energy on planning what you'll wear and shopping for it. In our society it's easy to worry so much about our clothes that they become idols and replace God as the focus of our lives. Remember Jesus' words in Matthew 6:25, 28–30:

So I tell you, don't worry about everyday life—whether you have enough food, drink, and clothes. Doesn't life consist of more than food and clothing? And why worry about your clothes? Look at the lilies and how they grow. They don't work or make their clothing, yet Solomon in all his glory was not dressed as beautifully as they are. And if God cares so wonderfully for flowers that are here today and gone tomorrow, won't he more surely care for you? You have so little faith. (NLT)

THE COMPANY PICNIC

If you're gearing up for your first company picnic, take a minute and browse through our helpful hints on what to do and what not to do. Even if you've been to so many picnics you've lost count, it might not be a bad idea to refresh yourself on some basic etiquette. We only have your best interests in mind!

WHAT TO DO

Picnic Games Gone Awry

"Last summer at my company picnic, we were practicing our golf swing and using marshmallows as golf balls. It was great fun until I twisted my knee so bad it swelled up like a melon. Two days later I had knee surgery. That's one picnic I'll never forget."
—Dave, Freeport, Maine

WOW!

1. Be sure to talk to your boss, and if possible, the CEO of the company.
Depending on the size of your company, you might have to reintroduce yourself to the head honcho, but don't shy away from this moment of opportunity to make a good personal impression.

2. Meet your coworkers' families.
This helps put names with faces when your coworkers talk about their spouses or children.

3. Talk about more than just work with your coworkers.

It's nice to get to know these people on a more personal basis. It might be awkward at first and just easier to talk about work, so come prepared in advance with topics and ideas to discuss. You'll be ready for any lulls in the conversation.

4. Be friendly and outgoing.

Even if this is hard for you, coax yourself out of that shell and go talk to someone you don't know very well.

5. Participate in the games or activities.

While you might feel stupid or afraid you'll make a fool out of yourself, try not to take yourself so seriously. You might actually have a good time playing.

WOW!

Top Five Worst Company Picnic Scenarios

5. You dressed in shorts and a T-shirt while everyone else showed up in business casual.
4. While running out of the rain, you got knocked out by a softball sized hail stone.
3. While bending over to pick up the volleyball, your shorts split wide open.
2. While talking with your boss you notice your three-and-a-half-year-old son using a tree as the bathroom.
1. You overhear your wife bragging to your boss about how you haven't been sick in two years, obviously forgetting you took a sick day last week.

6. Keep your kids in control.

Depending on their ages, you might want to consider taking things to keep your children occupied. And be sure to corral them before they get out of control. You don't want to be the one who ruins the picnic because your kids tipped over the food table while chasing each other.

7. Offer to cleanup.

Even if you know there's not much involved with cleanup, it is still nice to offer your service.

8. Be thankful.

Before leaving, be sure to thank your boss and those who coordinated the event. A thank-you card is a thoughtful gesture as well.

WHAT NOT TO DO

1. Don't hog the food.

We're not implying that you're some sort of farm animal hogging the trough, but we know how these events can get kicked off at an odd time, the caterer is late, or for some reason, you don't eat when expected. Then by the time you actually get to the food table, you're starving and ready to fill your plate a mile high. But take a deep breath and leave some for others. And be sure to wait to get seconds until everyone has had "firsts."

2. Don't brag about yourself to your boss.

Bragging is never a good idea, especially to your boss. He already knows how hard you've been working and the way you marvelously handled that last project, so keep your self praise to yourself.

3. Don't be cliquey.

It is so tempting to sit with your group of immediate coworkers and not interact with anyone else in the company. But take advantage of this time to get to know those whose faces you know but maybe have never said more than "hi" to.

DON'T BE SHY

Depending on your personality and whether you're an extrovert or an introvert, you may look forward to and enjoy the company picnic, or you may simply dread it. For all you shy folks who hate making small talk and just go to make an appearance and then leave, try to keep in mind that your company is hosting this event in appreciation of everyone and their hard work. So take a step back and instead of focusing so much on yourself, try to enjoy what they are doing for you. You might actually have a good time if you stay long enough!

THE COMMUTE

It's a cold, hard fact that everyone has to get to work some way or another. If you're one of those lucky people with a five-minute commute, count your blessings and try not to rub it in for the rest of us. But some of you might be commuting between one and four hours, which adds up to two to eight hours of travel time a day! That's a lot of time spent away from home, your family, your job, and not doing what you really want. So how do you manage the commute and keep from losing your mind? Read on.

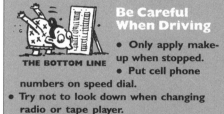

Be Careful When Driving

THE BOTTOM LINE

- **Only apply make-up when stopped.**
- **Put cell phone numbers on speed dial.**
- **Try not to look down when changing radio or tape player.**
- **Get regular car tune-ups.**
- **Join an auto club membership, like AAA or Shell Motor Club, to handle unexpected car problems.**

THE DRIVE

All of us at some point have gotten in the car and wondered how we were going to handle the long drive home after a hard day's work. The thought of battling traffic is enough to spark the search for a new job. But with a little thought and creativity, you *can* fight the driving blahs so you don't arrive home crabbier than when you left work. Try a few of these ideas and find what works for you.

1. Take this time to unwind.

Be up front with yourself that the traffic will be bad, and try to relax. Take some deep breaths and use this time to process the day's events or think about or plan other things. Remember, you can't control traffic, but you can control your emotions with regard to the traffic.

2. Do some work.

We're not advocating working on your laptop while swerving through traffic, but if possible, use this drive time to make and return phone calls. You might actually find yourself more productive during the day if you can save some of the calls for the drive home.

3. Listen to books on tape.

This could be the answer to never having enough time to read! Or you might consider learning a foreign language from tape. Check your local library.

4. Listen to favorite CDs and tapes.

Sometimes the radio just doesn't cut it, so be prepared with your favorite CDs or tapes.

5. Arrange to drive during off-traffic times.

If possible, rework your schedule so you can drive during off-traffic times. Afraid your boss won't let you veer from the 8 to 5 schedule? Asking is worth a try. Your company might be more flexible than expected, especially if you'll be putting in the same amount of time and your work doesn't suffer.

6. Pray.

If this is one of the few times of the day you have time alone, try using it to communicate with God.

I'M LATE, I'M LATE, FOR A VERY IMPORTANT DATE!

When you're running late, it never fails: You miss all the lights and then get behind the one car that's going slower than the speed limit. What is with that?! At any rate, you still need to drive carefully. It's tempting to speed, yield at stop signs, pretend that yellow light was yellow longer than it really was, and get all bent out of shape at drivers who are obeying the rules of the road. But realize that while all these attempts to get there faster might make you *feel* like you'll get there sooner, they usually don't work. Like when you speed to the next light, and the car behind arrives just in time for the green light while you sat there and waited. So take a deep breath and relax. You'll get there when you get there.

ROAD RAGE/DEFENSIVE DRIVING

When you were in high school, don't you remember your mom always saying, "Be careful!" every time you got in the car to drive somewhere? In reality, she wasn't as concerned about your driving as she was about the

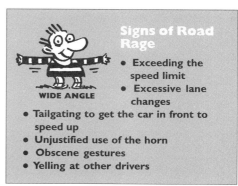

WIDE ANGLE

Signs of Road Rage

- Exceeding the speed limit
- Excessive lane changes
- Tailgating to get the car in front to speed up
- Unjustified use of the horn
- Obscene gestures
- Yelling at other drivers

other drivers on the road. Having been around the block a few more times than you, she knew people can drive like maniacs. Nowadays, that maniacal driving is called road rage, and it's something to watch out for. If you see anyone driving in this manner, get the license plate number and report it to the police.

CARPOOLS

While the thought of a carpool brings back memories of your mom driving the family wagon full of kids to soccer practice or cub scouts, don't disregard carpooling as only for kids. The same reasons the carpool works so well for moms makes it a great idea for getting to work.

- It saves money.
- It's less time spent behind the wheel and dealing with driving pressures.
- It's less miles put on your car.
- It's good for the environment. Less cars equal less pollution.
- It build friendships.

So find out where your co-workers live in proximity to you and work and figure out a way to carpool. It might be the stress relief you need!

Dry Run

If your commute requires driving or walking to the station, a train ride, and then a bus ride followed by more walking to your employment destination, it is imperative to do a dry run. You'd hate to arrive at work on a Monday morning an hour late because you couldn't find the bus stop, or the walk took longer than expected.

CATCH A CLUE

PUBLIC TRANSPORTATION

If you find yourself frequently banging on the steering wheel in frustration while your blood pressure soars through the roof, it's time to consider another medium to get to work. How about taking public transportation? Do you live or work near a bus route, the subway, a train or trolley system, or maybe a ferry? While riding, you can read, work, sleep, pray, listen to a

Walkman, or just unwind. But if you do decide to sleep, make sure you have a way of knowing when it's time to get off. Here's a true story about someone who missed his train stop.

"Instead of joining the mad rush to exit the train as it entered the Chicago terminal, I sat back and read my paper till the mob scene cleared out. After what seemed like only a minute, I collected my things, but when I stood up to leave, the lights and air conditioning went off! My heart started beating faster. I ran to the doors but they were locked, and the train was starting to move in the opposite direction—*away* from Chicago and from my work! As I ran through the cars to find someone, *anyone*, I realized I was the only person left on the train. After calling Metra on my cell phone and getting put on hold twice, I was told that the train was going to a train yard for maintenance. A half hour later it stopped in the yard and an engineer finally walked by and heard my pounding on the windows. After letting me out, he escorted me across a dozen tracks where I caught another train back into Chicago. Needless to say, I'm the first person off the train now!"
—Joel, Wheaton, Illinois

TRANSPORTATION ETIQUETTE

Unless you want to stand out like a neon sign blinking, "I've never ridden the train!" or "This is my first time on the subway!" take note of these unwritten rules.

- No matter how much your feet hurt, men should never wear walking shoes with suits. Women are exempt from this dress code.
- Always sit in the same seat.
- Never sit right next to someone you don't know. Leave an open seat between you.
- Don't talk to anyone, not even friends.

- Don't look at anyone else and *never* stare.
- Appear busy with your computer, phone, or newspaper.
- Flash your pass to the conductor. Never leave it out.
- Carry a travel mug of coffee. If you don't drink coffee, fill it with something to make it look like you do.
- Don't be late. Running for the train with your skirt hiked up and then to have it slammed in the door as it closes only creates a scene.

INCORPORATING EXERCISE

Sometimes all it takes to incorporate exercise into your commute is to get a little creative. To help stimulate your creative juices, ask yourself the following questions:

1. Could I walk to work?
2. Could I ride my bike to work?
3. Could I rollerblade to work?
4. Could I bike part way to work and then catch public transportation or drive my own car?
5. Could I walk part way to work and then catch public transportation or drive my own car?
6. Could I walk or bike to a train station farther away then the nearest one to my house and catch the train?

Before writing off number three or number four as an option, consider this fellow's commute:

"When I worked in downtown Chicago and lived in the suburbs, I'd bike fifteen miles on less-traveled roads to where I had parked my car. I would then drive the rest of the way to work and reverse the commute on the way home. It was great exercise, and I did it all year except when it was really, really cold." —Scott, Deerfield, Illinois

SECTION 11

GETTING YOUR ACT TOGETHER

FITTING IN EXERCISE

Unless your job is with an NBA team (as a player), a circus troupe, or a professional dance company, chances are you're going to need to find time to get some physical exercise.

You need to be getting the old bod in motion. And we don't just mean lifting your coffee mug or running after a glazed doughnut in the break room. We're talking good old-fashioned exercise here—stretching, sweating, and moving.

Regular exercise is a good thing. If you don't believe it, just sneak into your local cardiac unit and look at the folks who might not be there if they had bothered to maintain some semblance of physical fitness. Or better yet, flip through your TV channels late at night and watch all the powerful infomercials.

There are any number of ways you can pursue a healthier you. For only 120 easy payments of $79, you *could* buy that contraption that looks like a medieval torture device and that you'll eventually use for nothing more than a clothing rack in your bedroom. Or you can take a more reasonable approach.

Consider these possibilities:
- Utilize the company health club (only possible if you work for a big, Fortune 500 company; if your job is at Phil's Auto Salvage and Tatoo Parlor, the odds are you *probably* don't have this option).
- Join a health club near your place of employment (this way you can

workout before work, during the lunch hour, or on the way home each evening—instead of sitting in traffic fighting road rage).

- Buy a good pair of walking shoes and set your alarm thirty minutes earlier each morning. There's nothing like a brisk morning walk to wake you up and make you feel alive (and this can also double up as a good time to pray about the issues you'll be facing that day).
- Do the little things. If your job is sedentary and has you at your desk most of the day, take the stairs instead of the elevator. Take little breaks throughout the day to stand up and do some simple stretches or calisthenics, or to walk down the hall to say hello to a colleague, or to walk to lunch at a nearby restaurant (instead of driving).
- Make it a priority to do something physical as soon as you arrive home—wrestle with your kids on the living room floor or take your kids for a bike ride around the block.

The point is to do SOMETHING every day, to keep moving. As a recent commercial pointed out, "A body at rest tends to remain at rest; a body in motion tends to remain in motion."

Fight the tendency to be lethargic. You'll be healthier, happier, and have a much lower clothing bill!

MAKING BUDGETS

Let's talk about budgets.

Yeah, yeah, we know. This is *not* a fun topic. In a perfect world, we'd work for a boss with Bill Gates' resources and Santa Claus' personality. We'd have more money than we knew what to do with. We could spend without thinking. We'd never have to bother with records or expense accounts. But now we really *are* in dreamland. Back to reality. . . .

Though the concept of budgeting may *seem* odious and hateful, though it *sounds* oppressive and confining, budgets, when understood and implemented, can be quite liberating.

They free us from the relentless pressure to purchase every product that every salesman pitches to us. They free us from the heavy burden of wondering how we are going to make a profit. They free us from having to worry about angry managers and exasperated accountants.

In truth, there's probably no area in our working lives where we can shine for Christ more than in this area of handling our employer's financial assets. We want to be good stewards. We want to be totally aboveboard. We want to help our companies succeed and be profitable. How better to do that than to work hard to devise wise financial plans and then to work even harder to carry them out?

Since every company is different and no two go about this process in the same fashion, it's impossible in three pages to give comprehensive budgetary advice that covers every situation. However, there are some broad principles you would be wise to follow:

1. Pray.

As a believer in Christ and as one who seeks to honor God, you'll need wisdom as you make decisions involving large sums of money, and as you interact with lots of different personalities with lots of different ideas about how to proceed.

2. Gather as much data as you can.

Do your research. Review past records and future company goals. Reread memos. Double-check with your superiors to make sure you are clear on policies and procedures.

3. Involve all the necessary parties.

Do you know the old saying, "Hell hath no fury like a woman scorned"? Well, there's another saying, not quite so well-known but just as true, that goes like this: "Hades has no wrath like a colleague who is cut out of the loop."

Valuable Assets

CATCH A CLUE

Dilbert's pointy-haired boss (speaking to a group of employees): "I've been saying for years that 'employees are our most valuable asset.' It turns out that I was wrong. Money is our most valuable asset. Employees are ninth."

Employee: "I'm afraid to ask what came in eighth."

Boss: "Carbon paper."

What that means, in case you skipped your college classes in Shakespeare, is that you want to make sure that everybody who needs to be involved is consulted and has a chance to give input into the budget process. This increases your chances of having a budget that the troops will rally behind and work to carry out.

4. Be flexible.

Be a good listener. Try to see things from different perspectives. Don't cave in when you have a good idea, but also don't be stubborn. Remember, the point isn't to ramrod your own ideas about the budget through all the necessary channels; it is, rather, to find the best financial plan you can find.

5. Be a person of integrity.

Live in such a way that your bosses, colleagues, and/or underlings will be able to find nothing objectionable or questionable about your handling of company funds.

This Little Light of Mine. . .

THE BIBLE SAYS

"Let your light shine before men, that they may see your good deeds and praise your Father in heaven."
(Matthew 5:16)

ARRANGING YOUR SCHEDULE

Most workers (except for—*if* you believe the hype—the Maytag repairman) have to juggle lots of responsibilities and deadlines and assignments. Colleagues, bosses, clients—you name it, but they all want something, and most of them want it yesterday. Your inbox and mailbox and E-mailbox keep *filling up*, faster than you can *keep up*. And who has time to *catch up*, since most of our working lives are spent in meetings?!

The truth is all of us could stand to become more adept at time management so that we can get done all the things that scream for our attention.

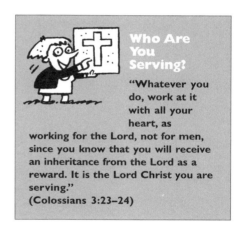

Who Are You Serving?

"Whatever you do, work at it with all your heart, as working for the Lord, not for men, since you know that you will receive an inheritance from the Lord as a reward. It is the Lord Christ you are serving."
(Colossians 3:23–24)

SOME TIME MANAGEMENT BASICS

- Purchase and utilize some kind of daily planner/appointment book and/or "to do" list. A wide selection of these are available at office supply stores as well as big chain stores like Wal-Mart, K-Mart, or Target.

- Make sure your planner includes a long-range calendar.
- Make it your practice to write down all upcoming deadlines, meetings, and appointments.
- Review your personal planner each afternoon or evening to get a sense of what you need to accomplish the next day.
- Prioritize the things you need to do. Which items are most important? Which ones could wait, if need be?

Beware of what one man has called "the tyranny of the urgent." This is the common phenomenon in which *urgent* things (e.g. deadlines, rush projects) tend constantly to swallow up all your time and energy so that you don't ever get around to *important* things.

Let's say you're a secretary who has to get out a regular, big bulk mailing. This would be an example of an *urgent* assignment for you. But if you installed and learned to use a new database software program that could save you lots of time and trouble on future mailings, that would be an example of an *important* task.

THE BOTTOM LINE

In Other Words. . .

In response to those cheesy inspirational posters that are often hung in businesses, someone has offered the following sayings for consideration:

Doing a job **RIGHT** the first time gets the job done. Doing the job **WRONG** fourteen times gives you job security.

Rome did not create a great empire by having meetings; they did it by killing all those who opposed them.

Never put off until tomorrow what you can avoid altogether.

We waste time, so you don't have to.

When the going gets tough, the tough take a coffee break.

Aim Low, Reach Your Goals, Avoid Disappointment.

We waste more time by 8:00 in the morning than other companies do all day.

Important tasks are seldom mandatory or tied to the clock. This is why they often get brushed aside. If all we do is react to urgent demands, our jobs take on an air of drudgery and stress; it's when we tackle important needs that we feel a sense of long-term impact.

- ***Make a plan for the next day's work.***
  Build at least thirty minutes of "fudge time" into your daily routine so that when an unexpected interruption occurs (and it will; they always do), you'll have time to deal with it without feeling stressed and rushed. (If no interruptions occur, you can use this "extra" time to get ahead on an upcoming project!)

- ***First thing in the morning review your daily schedule or "to do" list.***

Karoshi

At a departmental meeting, Dilbert's pointy-haired boss gives the following speech:

WOW!

"In Japan, employees occasionally work themselves to death. It's called *karoshi*. I don't want that to happen to anybody in my department. The trick is to take a break as soon as you see a bright light and hear dead relatives beckon."

- ***Pray.***
  . . .for the grace and discipline and discernment to work in a way that pleases and honors God.

- ***Utilize the extra moments.***
  Maintain a punch list of quick items (return phone calls, memos, notes, expense reports, etc.) that you can do in those normally "lost moments" waiting in traffic, waiting for appointments, waiting for meetings to begin. Keep your cell phone, beeper, planner, and laptop with you at all times. (And just think, by lugging all these gadgets around, you're

getting some great exercise—the subject of a previous chapter!)

- ***Cluster certain responsibilities.***
  By grouping certain assignments or errands you can eliminate extra trips or phone calls or the need to call additional meetings. Again, the key here is planning ahead. If you know you've got ten minutes with a VP who's in town, take some time to think through every question you need clarified on every project you're working on. Don't go into meetings half-cocked or take off down the hall without organizing yourself.

- ***Minimize "goofing off."***
  Lengthy personal discussions around the water cooler, personal phone calls, daydreaming, playing computer games, wandering the halls—all of these common habits can eat away at your schedule. Without a strong commitment to discipline, you can end up at the end of the day (or the week) with very little to show for your efforts.

DECISION-MAKING

If you're a corporate CEO, you make big decisions about mergers and layoffs and restructuring. If you're a hack in some gloomy cubicle on the seventeenth floor, you probably make decisions about which drawer (of two) in which to stash your paper clips.

But the point is that *every* worker makes decisions. And so the obvious question is, how do we make good decisions?

GENERALLY UNWISE DECISIONS

- Dating a coworker
- Dating your boss
- Dating an employee
- Calling old friends on the company's 800 line
- Repainting your office in your school colors without permission
- Sending off-color E-mail jokes to your humorless human resources director
- Auctioning off your department's computers on E-bay
- Grilling porkribs for lunch on a Hibachi in the lobby

SEVEN STEPS FOR MAKING DECISIONS

1. Pray.

You may be tired of hearing us encourage the practice of prayer, but the truth is that Christians *are* representatives of Christ in the workplace. Others are watching you. And so you want to be careful to portray a positive image of integrity and excellence. A foolish choice here, a whole series of unwise decisions there, and people will look with disdain upon you, and more importantly, upon your God.

Plans

"Make plans by seeking advice."

(Proverbs 20:18)

THE BIBLE SAYS

2. Gather all the necessary data.

Someone has said that when the facts become clear, the right choice becomes obvious. It's true! You need good info to make good decisions.

3. List the pros and cons.

If you have several options, take a few moments to consider the upside and downside of each potential choice. Think. Consider the past. Have there been similar situations previously? What decisions were made? What happened? Use common sense. Write it all down. Analyze it.

4. Solicit wise counsel.

Talk with peers you respect. Talk to those under you (this will usually endear them to you and make them more loyal since they feel re-spected and consulted). Depending on the magnitude of the decision, get input from your boss.

5. *Pull the trigger.*

Don't stress. Don't work yourself into a frenzy. When you've studied the situation carefully and considered all the options (as well as the likely outcomes), make a decision and don't look back.

6. *Take responsibility.*

What if you make a poor decision? (Actually the question isn't "if" but "when.") What do you do in those times? Resist the urge to blame or rationalize or justify. Be a stand-up guy or

More Inspirational Posters We'd Like to See

WOW!

Eagles may soar, but weasels don't get sucked into jet engines

A person who smiles in the face of adversity. . .probably has a scapegoat.

If you can stay calm, while all around you is chaos. . .then you probably haven't completely understood the situation.

If at first you don't succeed, try management.

TEAMWORK. . .means never having to take all the blame yourself.

Never underestimate the power of very stupid people in large groups.

INDECISION is the key to FLEXIBILITY.

gal. If in retrospect, your reasoning was flawed and your decision was a mistake, admit it. Apologize to those affected. If the decision can be revoked, do so. If not, work to minimize the damage.

7. *Learn from both your good and bad choices.*

In every situation there are lessons to be found. Keep a file (at least a mental one) of what worked and what didn't. Consult these "notes" before making future decisions.

WHAT DOES IT TAKE?

It takes more than expensive clothing and a good haircut to be successful in the corporate world. You also need to be the CEO's son or daughter-in-law.

Heh, heh. A little workplace humor there for you (and we emphasize the word "little"). But seriously, we all want to succeed in our chosen careers. We want to do a good job and feel productive and make a difference. We want to be assets to our employers.

How can we do that? Here are three phrases for you to tuck away:

EXERCISE INITIATIVE

The world is full of weasly employees who do just enough to get by. They sit back passively and wait for edicts from on high. Then they grudgingly, half-heartedly begin carrying out orders. Mediocre. Surly. Uninspired. Blah. That's what most of these folks

WOW!

Corporate Inefficiency, B.C.

"We trained hard, but every time we began to form up teams, we would be reorganized. I was to later learn in life that we tend to meet any new situation by reorganizing; and a wonderful method it can be for creating the illusion of progress while producing confusion, inefficiency, and demoralization."
—**Petronius Arbiter, 210 B.C.**

are (and if they skipped work for a month, it would demonstrate how unnecessary many of them are).

Most businesses are looking for employees with energy and initiative. Now by this, we're *not* suggesting that you take it upon yourself to be a corporate maverick who launches out with your own agenda/business plan. We *are* saying that you'll go farther in your job if you demonstrate a real concern for your company's success. Most bosses like workers who are constantly thinking about ways to improve the bottom line, who see needs and meet them, or see problems and fix them, without having to be told.

Find out what your boundaries are. Ask questions to ascertain the limits of your authority. And then, without overstepping your bounds, do everything you can to increase productivity, morale, and profits.

True Today

Though the original audience was slave laborers, the principle still applies today: "Slaves, obey your earthly masters in everything; and do it, not only when their eye is on you and to win their favor, but with sincerity of heart and reverence for the Lord." (Colossians 3:22)

SUBMIT TO AUTHORITY

Whether you blame it on Dr. Spock, the Woodstock generation, or television programming, the fact is that in this day and age "respect for authority" is a concept near extinction.

Whereas employers and bosses used to be venerated and feared, now they are cursed at, punched, and sued.

We're *not* suggesting absolute unquestioned obedience. But we *are* reminding you that it is honoring to God to submit to your superiors (as long as they don't require you to do something immoral, illegal, or unbiblical). You need to display respect. You need to be courteous. You need to go against the flow of your culture and refuse to participate in office conversations or activities that undermine your employer.

DISPLAY CONFIDENCE

Don't be a sniveling "brown noser" or "boot-licker." Don't be a door mat. Don't be paralyzed by indecision. On the contrary, use your strengths and gifts and experience to do the best job you can. If you DO feel inadequate doing a certain task, do all that you can (taking a class, bringing work home, asking for training) to get up to speed. Master areas of weakness.

Remember, no one respects a weak person. In fact, in the workplace/business world, coming across as an insecure pushover, is like bleeding in front of a school of hungry sharks. You'll get eaten alive!

LIFE OUTSIDE OF WORK

The story is told of an employee who came early and stayed late every single day. He outperformed all his fellow workers. He never complained, never missed a deadline, never missed work due to illness. He was a tremendous asset to his company.

One day, after a quarter of a century of faithful service, he called the office right at 8 A.M. to inform his employer that he had a terrible case of the flu. On the other end of the phone line, the boss exploded: "Oh, that's just great! Do you mean to tell me we're going to have to put up with this kind of thing every twenty-five years?!?!"

The working world can be cruel, eh? Sometimes companies want more than your honest labor. They want your heart, your soul, and all your waking hours.

This mentality of "being married to one's job" is unhealthy. It's not right. It's destructive.

Whether you're married or single, young or old, male or female, you need a life outside of work.

Priorities

"Nobody on his deathbed ever says, 'I wish I had spent more at the office'."

Attributed to Peter Lynch, former manager of the Fidelity Magellan fund

WOW!

Here are eight principles to latch on to whenever work is becoming all-consuming. (And to help you remember them, we've put them in the acronym **G-E-T A L-I-F-E**!)

Get God's perspective each and every day.

Whether you call it a "quiet time" or a "devotional," you need some time each day with God in His Word. You need to still your soul and remember the things that are true above all else. You need to recall that we were put on this earth to love and honor and serve God and others, not to pursue a career. This daily appointment with God is a touchstone with reality and eternity. It can keep you thinking straight in a twisted world.

Evaluate regularly.

It was Socrates who said, "The unexamined life is not worth living." (Whoa! No wonder everyone considered him such a wise guy!) Doesn't it make sense to take stock often of your life—where you've been, where you're going? If you don't pause to check your course, how can you know if you're on the right track? Schedule an evening or a Saturday or a whole weekend at least twice a year to huddle with your spouse and ask yourselves hard questions like: How are we doing? Is this where God wants us? What is our current lifestyle (including work) doing to our marriage, our family, our church involvement?

Take up a hobby.

It's true: All work and no play makes Jack a dull boy (and Jackie a really ticked-off girl!). You *need* an outlet: fishing, hunting, hiking, golf (on second thought, golf may actually increase your stress level!), tennis, birdwatching, gardening, woodworking, etc. Find *something* to do that fits your personality and that has a soothing, therapeutic effect on you. You want a hobby that restores and replenishes you emotionally, not one that leaves you drained.

Address inequities.

If the demands of your job are unrelenting and unfair, speak up. Do so gently and with respect. But if you're a hard-working, faithful employee who's doing a good job, you have every right to draw some boundaries. We can hear some readers saying: *I can't do that! I might lose my job!* True, but did you ever think about *these* questions: "What if you lose your mind? Or your marriage? Or your kids?" Is a grueling, grinding job worth all that? Hey, there are other jobs you can do without having to work for Attila the Hun!

Leave your work at work.

Every evening on his way home, one man goes through the mental exercise of dumping all his work-related headaches and projects and pending decisions along the expressway (near a certain mile marker). In the morning on his commute back to work, he mentally picks them up. He is committed to NOT bringing all that junk into his home and letting it intrude on his family time. A wise practice!

Invite accountability.

Ask a friend or two to ask you hard questions about your tendency to overwork. (It's probably better if it's not your spouse!) Give your friend(s) permission to "kidnap" you when you're being a workaholic and to deliver you to your family or to force you to engage in your hobby.

Face up to dead-end situations.

It's a scary place to be, but every now and then you could find yourself working in a job that shows no prospect of getting better. It's a stressful, dead-end situation. It's taking a toll on your gut and on your family. If you're in this place, you may need to lose your job to save your life.

Enjoy time off.

Take full advantage of every holiday, every vacation day, even your lunch breaks. Savor those times. Relish the opportunity to be with family and friends. If you find it difficult to let work go and unwind, we highly recommend an older book by Tim Hansel called *When I Relax I Feel Guilty*.

MAINTAINING FRIENDSHIPS

Years ago the Beatles moved a whole generation when they sang those immortal lyrics:

"I am the eggman, they are the eggman, I am the walrus, goo goo goo joob."

Whoops! Wrong song there. What the Beatles *actually* sang was a mournful melody called "Eleanor Rigby" which included the refrain: "Ah, look at all the lonely people!"

Lonely people. *Lots* of them. And if it was true then, it's even more so today. We live in a culture of distrust and distance. The number of singles grows. Our expressways are filled with solitary commuters. Office parks are jammed with colleagues who keep each other at arm's length.

We **NEED** Other People!

"**Two are better than one, because they have a good return for their work: If one falls down, his friend can help him up. But pity the man who falls and has no one to help him up!**" (Ecclesiastes 4:9–10).

The end result? Isolated people with few deep interpersonal connections.

This trend doesn't make for a very satisfying workplace situation. In fact, this kind of existence *can* breed a kind of despair.

The Bible states in the opening chapter that we bear "the image of

God" (Genesis 1:26–28). What does this mean? Well, orthodox Christian teaching states that though God is *One*, He exists eternally in *three* Persons—Father, Son, and Holy Spirit—who live in perfect relationship with each other. Thus, bearing the image of God would seem to indicate that we too are meant to live in relationship. Indeed, we were designed by our Creator to love, serve, interact, listen, give, submit, encourage, share, cooperate, confront, hug, sympathize, etc. (and to receive those things in return).

In short we need friends. We need them both in the workplace and outside our jobs.

FRIENDSHIPS IN THE WORKPLACE

These kinds of relationships can be tricky because colleagues can often be insecure, competitive, and petty. It's not uncommon for people to use other people in a desperate attempt to climb higher in the corporate pecking order.

So, we won't lie to you—pursuing friendships in the office can be risky. You can get stabbed in the back. You can be betrayed. Nevertheless, it honors God when we move toward others with the purpose of blessing them and seeking their good.

Some truths to remember

- You can't be best buddies with everyone. Deep friendship requires lots of time and effort. We can, however, be *friendly* to everyone.
- Christ is our model of friendship. He loved unconditionally and forgave others lavishly. (Forgiveness is perhaps the most important, most

needed factor in office friendships—or *any* relationships, for that matter!)

- Christ alone can meet our deepest emotional needs. It's a mistake for us to look to another human to fill the holes in our souls that only God can fill.
- Only as we are trusting fully in Christ—in His absolute love, in His promise to be with us always, in all of His infinite resources of joy and peace, etc.—will we have the confidence and security to approach others with no agenda other than to befriend them.
- Many people, out of suspicion and fear and because of past hurts, will resist our efforts to be friendly. Nothing we do can convince them that we really have their best interests at heart. Do not let this discourage you. Just continue to show love, keep praying, and perhaps over time, God will change that hard and/or wounded heart.

Some wise warnings to tuck away

- Be professional. Make sure that your friendship doesn't cause you to goof off on the job. It's possible to find another person with whom you really hit it off, and when you do, your performance can suffer. Keep in mind that you've been hired first and foremost to do a job, not to hang out with a buddy or two.
- Be careful. There's nothing "wrong" about being close to another worker or two, just make sure you don't cause others to feel excluded. Don't be cliquish. This can poison an office environment quicker than anything.
- Be proactive. If you develop a close friendship with someone on the job, talk about the issues raised by this development. Draw some boundaries and ground rules. Otherwise, you may one day find yourselves unprepared to deal with a situation where there are serious differences at work.

FRIENDSHIPS OUTSIDE THE WORKPLACE

An upside to having friends on the job is that you have a lot in common. You've "gone to war" together—tackling projects or wooing and satisfying clients. These shared experiences can often form deep bonds.

But this same positive can also be a negative. The drawback to having friends *only* at work is that you often end up talking only about work-related issues. Even when you're having lunch with that friend or shopping or playing golf together, you never really get away from the office.

This is why it's a good idea to have friends outside the workplace.

To find friendships outside your place of work

- You'll have to make people a priority.
- You'll have to take the initative.

CATCH A CLUE

Greener Pastures

"When we moved from sprawling Atlanta to a small town in Louisiana, I relished the thought of no rush-hour traffic, less crime, a more family-oriented community, and a slower pace of life. I had this mental image of living on a quiet cul-de-sac. And in that picturesque neighborhood, kids rode bikes and built tree houses together. Relaxed wives sipped tea and visited on porch swings. The men gathered regularly to barbecue and watch football. Maybe I'd seen one Norman Rockwell painting too many.

"Anyway, what I discovered was that even though our new community is small and friendly and a wonderful place to rear children, people are still busy. Little leagues, church stuff, family obligations. Connecting with guys here is just as difficult as anywhere!

"My conclusion: Friendship takes effort and work. It seldom *just happens.*"
—**Woody, 40, Ruston, Louisiana**

- You'll have to set aside time to be with others.
- You'll have to both talk and LISTEN. Communication is the lifeblood of good relationships.
- You'll have to treat people the way you want to be treated.
- You'll have to persevere. Friendships take time to develop and mature.

Simple, friendly gestures that can lead to friendships

- Invite someone to play golf or go shopping or fishing.
- Join a couples class at church.
- Have another family over for lunch after church.
- Offer to drive another couple to the next Parent-Teacher meeting at your kids' school.
- Invite a neighbor over for coffee and dessert.
- Ask an acquaintance to help you coach a little league team.
- Invite the new couple over for barbecue.
- Ask that person who's an "expert" to help you with a project.
- Offer your expertise to a neighbor you'd like to get to know.

WOW!

Wise Words About Friendship!

"Friendship improves happiness and abates misery, by the doubling of our joy and the dividing of our grief."
—Marcus Tullius Cicero

"Is any pleasure on earth as great as a circle of Christian friends by a good fire?"
—C. S. Lewis

"If I had to give a piece of advice to a young man about a place to live, I think I should say, 'Sacrifice almost everything to live where you can be near your friends.'"
—C. S. Lewis

FINDING A MENTOR

The concept of mentoring has become a hot topic in business circles in the last few years. (A mentor being defined as: "a trusted counselor or guide, a tutor or coach.")

With all the hype, one would think mentoring is a brand-new idea. It's not. As Ted Engstrom has said: "[Up until this century] mentoring—the development of a person—was a way of life between the generations. It was to human relationships what breathing is to the body. Mentoring was assumed, expected, and, therefore, almost unnoticed because of its common-ness in human experience."

My, how times have changed! Instead of apprenticeships and long-term, comprehensive one-on-one training and modeling, we now quickly herd people like cattle through large impersonal educa-

Dilbert the Mentor

wow!

Dilbert demonstrates for us how **NOT** to mentor someone.

(Standing behind a new employee): "This is your computer."

(Grabbing the employee's computer mouse): "When you hear footsteps it's a good idea to move this thing around and click it."

(Walking away): "This concludes your technical training. If you have further questions just remember you're inconveniencing me."

tional or technical institutions. They get lectures, go to seminars, and read textbooks, but there's precious little hands-on experience. Rarely do they get to watch a master at his or her craft. Gone are the non-rushed settings where deep insights and profound life lessons are passed on.

The result is that we now live in a society of people who possess lots of information, but very little wisdom. And so there's a need for models, for older and wiser and more experienced people to come alongside younger folks and help show them the way.

WHAT CONSTITUTES A GOOD MENTOR?

- **Someone with character**
  Many in our culture have accepted the pop notion that "character doesn't matter, only job performance." Nothing could be further from the truth. As Nathaniel Hawthorne so wisely noted: "No man can for any considerable time wear one face to himself and another to the multitude without finally getting bewildered as to which is the true one." Since it's impossible to truly compartmentalize one's life (unless we are schizophrenic!), we must seek out (and be) mentors who have integrity.

- **Someone with skill and wisdom**
  A good mentor is good at what he does. He is marked by excellence. And this expertise has been rigorously developed and honed "down in the trenches." The best mentors are not theoreticians, but those who have been tested in the fire and trials of real life.

- **Someone with a desire to pass on what he/she knows**
  All the wisdom and experience in the world is worthless if the one who possesses it is unwilling to share it. The best mentors have a passion to pour themselves into others, to leave a legacy.

WHERE CAN ONE FIND A MENTOR?

Perhaps there is an older person in your place of employment who fits the criteria above. Maybe a retiree in your church or neighborhood would be willing to work with you. You might look to a parent, grandparent, or favorite aunt or uncle.

HOW DOES ONE "SECURE THE SERVICES OF A MENTOR"?

If you've identified a person you respect and think has much wisdom to share, approach him or her and say something like: "This may sound funny, but I really admire you and think you have a lot of personal and business wisdom. Would you be willing to meet with me (weekly/have lunch with me a couple times a month/get together monthly/take your pick) and let me pick your brain?"

What's the worst that can happen? He/she might say "no." On the other hand. . .

WORDS OF CAUTION

1. Don't look to a mentor to "fix" all your problems.
2. Don't look to a mentor to "tell you what to do" in every situation.
3. Don't feel that you must do everything your mentor advises. (Pray before decisions and seek God's counsel above all else.)
4. Don't try to *be* your mentor. (Remember God has made you unique and has a special plan just for you. Mentoring is *not* about trying to replicate the life experience of another.)

5. Don't become a nuisance or pest. (Respect that your mentor has a life!)
6. Don't forget to express appreciation.
7. Don't forget that there are younger folks whom YOU can mentor.

SECTION 12

······················

FAMILY

WAKING UP TO THE GRIND

"Daddy, I need a drink of water."

Your eyes finally adjust enough so you can get a glimpse of the clock. It's 5:30 A.M.

"Sweetie, we're all getting up in just thirty minutes. Can't you wait just a little while longer?"

"Okay."

But that wasn't the end of it. Just a few minutes later you're awakened by the sound of your same small child weeping. You lumber into her room where she's sitting up in bed sobbing.

"What's wrong?"

"Daddy, I really want a drink. And you said to wait. I don't want to wait. I'm thirsty."

"Well," you think to yourself, "I'm up anyway."

So, you go ahead and turn off the alarm and stagger down the stairs to get her a drink when a horrifying thought passes through your mind.

That report! I was supposed to have that report in today!

Instead of getting your daughter her drink, you head for your computer and begin typing. In an hour, you've got your notes strewn throughout the room. In two hours, you're printing the report.

"Time for a shower," you think to yourself. "I wonder why I'm not hearing everyone else. Hmm."

Passing through the bedroom, you see your wife still asleep. It's 7:30 A.M. The kids are late for school—in fact, they're not even awake!

So, the rush begins. Quick showers, fast breakfasts, sloppy clothes, and several rushed conversations with your spouse. The week begins.

Welcome to the race.

Managing your family and your job isn't easy. The pressure at work can feel out of this world. And, it's so easy to focus on your performance at work and miss making memories and moments with your family. We want you to take some time out and review your life with your family. Having trouble managing work and home? Failing at home, succeeding at work? Listing your priorities, but not living them?

Before you dive headfirst into this chapter, take a moment right now and consider the balance you're keeping between work and family. How are you doing? Where are you succeeding? Where do you need to grow? Consider these questions and write your responses in the spaces below.

- Areas I'm succeeding in keeping a healthy balance between work and family:

_____

- Areas I'm failing in keeping a healthy balance between work and family:

_____

- Now, take a moment and describe your typical week. List each day, and write out how much time your family gets from you and how much time you give to work.

_____

_____

This chapter is designed to encourage and challenge you. We want you to examine how you're managing your two very important worlds—home and work.

THE GREAT DIVORCE

Divorce can be a good thing.

Don't believe us?

Consider this. It's okay to divorce yourself from a threatening situation. Right? How about divorcing yourself from a friend who's trying to influence you away from God. Divorce is okay then, too.

It's okay to separate ourselves from things, places, and situations that are filled with opportunities to hurt us. We want you to gain a healthy sense of divorce. Not from your spouse, but from your work. Take a few moments and grade yourself and your ability to divorce yourself from work.

Thinking about separating your work and your personal life is a great idea. ANYONE can desire to make the separation, but how do you do it? First, let's look at why we tend to work extra hours and what motivates us to spend more time at work than with our families. As you read these, ask yourself, "Is this describing me?"

Workaholism
Some of us just can't stop working. When we leave the office, we feel an overwhelming sense of guilt because we're stepping away from work and possibly might be enjoying ourselves.

Needing to be needed
Getting emotional fulfillment from work is a dangerous thing. What happens when our work is substandard? How about when our performance is criticized? Some people stay at work because it fills an inner sense of being needed.

Quiz Time

Take this short quiz before you go any further. You can just circle your answers.

1. I feel guilty when I leave work unfinished at the office. This guilt often leads me to stay much later than I ought to.
Yes
No

2. There are days when I'm never present to put my children to bed.
Yes
No

3. I often work a full workday on Saturdays.
Yes
No

4. I rarely go out of my way to be home on time for evening meals.
Yes
No

5. My children comment about how often I'm absent from important family moments.
Yes
No

Now, take a moment to reflect:
- Too many "Yes's" and you've got a problem. We'll let you decide how many is too many. But if you've got more than one, you might need to think about divorcing yourself from work a little more.
- Too many "No's" is a good thing. If you answered all of the questions with a resounding "NO!" then you're on the right track. Great job!!

Overcommitment
It's difficult to say no to our bosses. It's difficult especially when they hold our jobs in the balance. Overcommitting isn't always our fault. Letting it go on and on *is* our fault. And, when we allow our work environment to control our activities with our family, we're in more danger than we think.

Overworked
If you work for a boss who can't stop giving you projects, you know all about being overworked. It might not be your fault that you have twenty-five things due this Monday morning. If you said no to any of them, you might have lost your job.

Greed
Sometimes, working extra hours, or another day means we can afford an extra payment. Or, often we need to work extra hours in order to pay for the things we've charged. Greed can lead us down a long road and trap us from our families.

Climbing the corporate ladder
Got your sites set on CEO? How about being the top secretary in the firm? Whatever your personal goal, it can be very easy to try and impress people by taking on extra work.

Hate being home?
For some people, staying at work all day every day means that they'll avoid a spouse, mother-in-law or other person they've grown to dislike. There are a lot of issues wrapped up in this one well beyond the scope of what we want to talk about. But if you can't stand being home, work often becomes the safe haven you need.

Desire to provide

Some people love providing for their families. That joy can lead them into working too much. It's one thing to love providing for our families. It's quite another when we allow our joy to create a wall between us and the people we love.

Did you see yourself in any of those short descriptions? You might have. If you did, write which one and why in the space below.

_____

_____

_____

_____

_____

_____

MAKING THE SEPARATION

No one knows your situation quite like you do. We all stay at the office for a variety of reasons. If you find yourself stuck in the rut of being at work more than at home, try some of these ideas to get yourself kick-started into a healthier family life.

NO!

Your first real, tangible step in getting ahold of yourself and your situation is by using that wonderful two letter word as often as you can. Begin by saying "no" to yourself. Tell yourself that you won't stay regardless of what comes up, who wants your help, and how good you'll feel piling another responsibility on yourself. Your first "NO" will feel really bad. In fact, you might feel downright rotten after you say it. But keep trying it out. Before too long, you'll get better at it, and you'll begin creating some much-needed space in your life.

FAMILY PICTURES

It might sound trivial, but keeping pictures of your family on your desk at work doesn't just serve as a great conversation starter with your co-workers. It also serves as a reminder. As you're working away at the office, take some time to look at those pictures. Ask yourself, "Do I really know these people?" or "Am I giving these people the best part of my day?" As you seek to answer those questions, God will begin to reveal to you what you need to do to re-connect with them. Keeping them present with you at work will allow you to keep them and your commitment to them at the front of almost every "work thought" you have.

FAMILY EVENTS

Your son's soccer competition is coming up. Your daughter has made it to the regional finals for the 440. Remember when those events will happen? How can you?

It's simple. Put every family event on your work schedule. Whether it's your wife's hair appointment or your husband's dentist visit—every family event ought to be on your work calendar. Doing this connects you to them when you're apart throughout the day. It also reminds you that they're real people with real things going on in their lives. Oh, and you'll probably not miss that recital, either.

DRIVING TO WORK

One of the best ways to protect yourself from piling too much on yourself is by deciding before you get to work what you'll do that day. Take some time at a stoplight or in the parking lot and make a few decisions:

- Decide that you'll leave on time.
- Decide that you'll not take any more work on that day.
- Decide what time you'll go home.
- Choose to walk into your home at the end of the day and leave work behind you.

DRIVING HOME

You've had an unbelievable day. The boss yelled. Your secretary yelled. A client yelled. You yelled—often at yourself. And, you got almost nothing done. Now you've got a choice. Open the door, say "hi," head for the bedroom and isolate yourself from everyone while you catch up, check your emotions, and meet a few deadlines.

Consider something else. Try taking an extra-long drive home. Remember that everything will be as you left it at work, and you probably won't get that much done at home anyway. As you drive home, try some constructive exercises that will prepare you to meet your family again, talk about their world, involve yourself in their lives, and create quality moments with them.

One good way to do this is to spend time praying. When you get in your car after a difficult day, take a few deep breaths, then begin with the words, "Dear Lord, Today I. . ." and continue telling God how your day made you feel (okay, so He already *knows* what happened today, but telling Him helps you, and it shows Him what's really on your mind). After you've told God about your day, tell Him that you need strength, help, and encouragement for the coming day.

If you're stuck about how to pray after a difficult day, try Reinhold Neibuhr's serenity prayer:

> *God grant me the serenity to accept the things I cannot*
> *change,*
> *the courage to change the things I can,*
> *and the wisdom to know the difference.*
> *Living one day at a time;*
> *Enjoying one moment at a time.*
> *Accepting hardship as the pathway to peace.*

Taking as He did, this sinful world as it is,
not as I would have it.
Trusting that He will make it right;
If I surrender to His will.
That I may be reasonably happy in this life,
and supremely happy with Him forever in the next.
Amen.
(Reinhold Neibuhr, 1926)

DITCH THE CASE

Your briefcase is something that represents your work. You probably keep important papers in it. There's significant company documents in it, notes for an upcoming project, or reports that need to be reviewed. However, all of those very important things that are work-related are like an anchor that's been handcuffed to your wrist. Everything in your briefcase serves one purpose—to keep you away from your family.

Now, getting rid of your briefcase might not be easy. Commit to leaving yours at work a few times each week for starters. Then, when you're comfortable, work toward never bringing it home. If you absolutely have to have it with you at all times, try leaving it in the car when you first get home. Take it out only after the kids are in bed, your spouse is willing to let you go get it, or you need something important from it.

EARLY BIRD WORK

Most quality family time happens in the evening. And, it's usually evenings that we're tempted to stay late. But, staying late isn't usually something that springs up at the last minute. Most of us know when we leave work the night before if the next day will be a late one. How do you get those extra hours in and still make room for the family?

Go in early. It might not be the easiest thing at first, but going in early will help you avoid staying late. Being at work early just might mean you'll avoid people for a few hours and will be able to get some important things accomplished without the normal office banter that usually occurs. If you do this, make sure that you get plenty of sleep the night before. Your work will be enhanced if you've had enough sleep, and you'll be ready for your family when you get home that night.

TAKE A QUICK CHECKUP...

We want you to take a moment and check yourself. After you've read all of the stuff we've written above, it's important to evaluate how you're doing with keeping your family a priority. So, give this book to your spouse and one family member (if you have another family member to give it to). Ask the following questions and have them write their answers below:

- Am I keeping the family a priority? If I'm not, please explain what you feel I'm doing incorrectly.

- Do you feel that you get the best of me every day? If you don't, tell me what you feel distracts me from paying closer attention to you.

MAKING THE RIGHT MOVES

So, you've blown it. Your family places your picture at your place at the table because you're never there. They've taken up the phrase, "And your name is. . . ?" every time you enter the room.

If you've succeeded in letting work creep in and take over your family life, it's time to take control again. We mentioned a lot of ideas for keeping work separate from home life already; your first step is to look to those ideas for ways to regain your life with your family.

Apologize

Your family might not believe it at first (especially if you've got a track record of doing this), but they deserve an apology. Be up front with your excuses about why you've put them on the back burner.

Reconstruct

Give them a plan for how you'll live your life differently. Your plan should include things like being home on time, being present for family events, or whatever else you've missed out on recently. Make your reconstruction steps specific and measurable. Instead of saying, "I'll be home more. I promise!" say something like, "I'll be home every evening at 5:30. You can expect it."

Safety net

Ask your spouse and children to be honest with you about how you're living up to your commitment. Put strategies in place to make sure you follow through with your commitment. You might want to have your spouse call you to remind you what time it is, or to tell you family events that need to go on the calendar.

Evaluate

Every month or so, step back and privately evaluate your performance. Are you living up to your expectations as a spouse and parent? Where are you missing the mark? Once you've evaluated, talk with your spouse about adjustments you'd like to make.

Maybe you're ready for a more drastic step. If you're looking for ways to get yourself reacquainted with your family, take some time to try one of these ideas.

WIDE ANGLE

Conversation Starters

So, you don't know what to talk about with your family? Try these conversation starters with your spouse and kids.

- **How was school/work?**
- **What did you learn today?**
- **What should we do for our family vacation?**
- **If you could be anyone in the world, who would you be? Why?**
- **What's your favorite TV show right now?**
- **When was the last time you laughed really loud?**

FAMILY NIGHTS, FAMILY DAYS

Many restaurants offer family night meals. They're the ones where kids eat free or at a discount when joined by their parents. Sure, they're still making a profit, but it's important for you to take advantage of this marketing strategy. But you don't have to just take them out for dinner. Schedule an entire day and go away somewhere.

At a loss for some creative ideas? Consider some of these family outings:

- Go putt-putting
- Go watch airplanes land
- Eat ice cream in the park
- Go to the mall and window-shop
- Wash the car
- Give each family member a dollar and buy each other something at a discount store
- Sit in the middle of the living room and stare at each other
- Rent a movie together—and watch it together
- Go for a drive
- Go for a walk
- Wash the dog
- Mow the lawn
- Shovel the snow

Those are just a few ideas. The key is to pick something everyone can get in on and do it. And don't feel guilty if you can't get everyone in on the action at first. Keep working at it. If you keep doing fun things, everyone will want to get in on the action.

FAMILY VACATIONS

Having fun together is the best way to reconnect with your family. Had a vacation lately? Enjoyed a roller coaster with your kids?

The best way to get started on a family vacation is to plan one. Tell your boss when you're taking it, put it on every calendar you've got, and then begin making reservations. Buy equipment. Get brochures. Surf Web pages looking for more information. And, be sure to plan times when you'll sit down with your family and just talk. Plan to get away from the hype of the amusement park, find a quiet place and talk about how you're feeling. Remember this: Getting a family vacation off the ground is much more difficult than following through with it. So, begin talking about it now. Once you've talked about it for awhile, the rest of your family will expect it, talk about it with their friends, and soon it'll become something everyone's excited about.

Another important family event that's not necessarily "fun"-related is a family retreat. It's important to take time apart from your weekly activities with your family and spend time in "spiritual" bonding.

Here are some ideas:

- Visit a monestary.
- Attend a church other than the one you're used to. When the service is over, talk about what you learned and how the service was different from what you're used to.
- Take a faith walk. Lead the family in a blindfolded walk through the neighborhood. When the walk is over, discuss the level of faith you all have.
- Go on a family campout. Ask each family member to prepare a short testimony about his or her life with Jesus up to this point. Spend evenings around a campfire singing and praying.

KIDS AT WORK

You've realized that the separation that work has created between you and your family is serious. You need time with your kids. How do you do that?

If you've tried the other ideas and you're looking for some more options, you might consider bringing them to work with you. Use these general guidelines to help you if you're considering bringing your children to work with you.

DO'S

Boss's day off
We aren't encouraging you to be sneaky, but you might want to wait to take your kid to work when your boss is out of town or has the day off. This will ensure that they won't get in the boss's way, and you won't be portrayed as someone who's just marking time with your kid at work.

Getting permission
If you've faced a serious scheduling conflict and you have to take your kid to work with you, be sure to get permission from your boss. Asking in advance portrays you as a committed worker *and* a caring parent.

Projects
If you've got a smaller child, bring coloring books, child protective scissors and paper, puzzles, and other projects for him to work on. Older children

might not need much supervision, but you'll still need to provide them with some projects to keep them busy.

Older children especially like the adventure of being at their parent's workplace. If your boss allows, you might want to let them wander through the building just looking around. And, if they're willing, have your child run office errands for you like taking things to be copied, delivering memos, or arranging the company break room.

Introduce your child

It's often easy to forget that you've got your child at work and focus on your work activities. However, when you take your child to work you've got an incredible opportunity to introduce your child to your world away from home. As she is working with you, introduce her to people who stop by your desk to talk shop.

Take advantage of the moment

Having your child at work with you is an opportunity to get to know more about him. If you've got your kid at work, plan a special lunch with him, take breaks every now and then to show him your favorite parts of the building or a messy drawer with interesting office gadgets you never use.

DON'T

Substitute

Taking your children to work with you is not a substitute for spending time with them. If you take them to work with you, then ignore them at home, you're really not accomplishing anything. Go ahead and take your child to work, but then continue your normal routine at home.

Busy days

It's not smart to take your child to work with you when you've got a busy day that includes meetings or one requiring extra concentration.

Get impatient

Working and parenting at the same time can be a harrowing experience. It's easy to get frustrated. Losing your temper might just happen when you're not expecting it. If something happens—your child tips over the printer or a customer loses his patience, don't lose it with your child. She'll learn a lot about work, and how to handle stress, from watching you. So, be a role model as much as you can.

BEST FRIENDS AND WORKMATES

It's 5:30. Quitting time.

You walk out of your office, give your secretary a hug and a quick smooch. Then, you help her on with her coat and head out the door. And, no one bats an eye. Because the secretary is your spouse.

If you work with your spouse, you know that you've entered one of the most challenging aspects of life together. Establishing your home was difficult enough. Raising kids wasn't easy either. But working together is a new, uncharted territory. How can you work together with your spouse and maneuver around the various troubling pylons you'll encounter?

Long ago, the apostle Paul saw this coming. He might not have envisioned couples working together in the workplace, but he had a good knowledge of what makes a marriage work regardless of the circumstances. His words ring true today.

"Wives, submit to your husbands as to the Lord. For the husband is the head of the wife as Christ is the head of the church, his body, of which he is the Savior" (Ephesians 5:22–23).

"Husbands, love your wives, just as Christ loved the church and gave himself up for her to make her holy, cleansing her by the washing with water through the word, and to present her to himself as a radiant church, without stain or wrinkle or any other blemish, but holy and blameless. In this same way, husbands ought to love their wives as their own bodies" (Ephesians 5:25–28).

After reading those passages from Ephesians, what do you notice about how you might work better with your spouse? Take a moment and write your thoughts on the lines provided.

GOD'S HELP FOR WORKING TOGETHER

Paul's words ring true today because they're simple and God-centered. Here's a snapshot of what he's getting at in these verses.

Love

Your relationship with your spouse must be filled with love. How does that translate into your work environment? Everything you do together or *to* each other at work must be loving. Leaving a message for him? End it with an "I love you." Talking with her about an important project? Put your hand on her back as a loving gesture of your affection. Others will see your loving acts and admire them. And, the loving acts will encourage the love relationship outside your work environment.

Sacrifice

Paul's encouragement is also one of sacrifice. He's urging us to give up our lives for our spouses. So, how does that translate into the work environment?

Help your spouse with those important projects. Work hard for him to succeed—even above your own success. When you *don't* agree on things at the office, be the one who will give in and let him have his way. Paul is urging us not to work for furthering our own ideas, projects, or interests. Paul is encouraging us to consider our spouses above ourselves—in everything we do.

Teamwork

Paul's description goes beyond the simple work relationship and describes a relationship where the two of you are on the same team.

Paul's encouragement might transform modern coworking couples' mindsets. He's asking us to view our lives together as people who are attempting to achieve the same end result. Mutual love. Furthering the gospel. Modeling a healthy marriage. How do you do that at work?

- Wear the same shirt. One day a week or month, both of you wear the same shirt, pants, or socks.
- Out for lunch. Take another coworking couple out for lunch with you.
- Model criticism. When your spouse criticizes you about something, receive it amicably.
- Respect. Don't abuse the others' work space, leaving items there that you would want in your office space. Don't volunteer the other for tasks at the office that you don't want to do.
- Pray together. Model teamwork by publicly praying in your office before the day begins. Pray for your children. Pray for your work day. And, pray for each other.
- Love each other. God's people, and God's couples, are known for their love for each other. So, spend every moment at work striving to love each other. Love in the way you deliver messages, work through projects, and interact with each other's friends. You'll not only demonstrate whose team you're on, you'll infect where you work with Christ's love.

INDEX

adversity 120

annoying habits 49

benefits 166

birthdays 64

boss 12, 23, 59

break room 52

budgets 192

caring for employees 66

carpools 186

casual Friday 176, 177

Christian witness 81

clothing 51, 173

commuting 183, 227, 228

company parties 64

company picnic 179

confidence 204

confrontation 123

conscience 146

contentment 152

coworkers 16, 23

cubicle 44

dating 22, 23

deadlines 132

decision-making 199

decorating a cubicle 46

difficult coworker 20

discrimination 127

dress code 51, 173

Email 41

employer 12, 59

ethics 135

etiquette 41, 50, 187

evaluations 54, 68

executive summary 36

exercise 188, 190

expense accounts 142

family 2, 65, 219, 226, 231

following directions 14

friendships 209

fruit of the Spirit 77

fulfillment 8

getting to know your employees   60

initiative 202

integrity 144

intra-office dating 22

kids at work 235

late 185

lunch break 170

management styles 12

market value 55

meetings 51

mentor 214

multimedia 39

performance reviews 54, 68

presenting reports 36

priorities 2, 6, 205

progress reports 15

public transportation 186

quality time 2, 4, 5, 7

raises 55, 72, 164

reports 15, 36

retirement 161

reviews 54, 68

road rage 185

salary 164

satisfaction 8

saving 159

schedules 195

schmoozing 15

sharing a cubicle 47

spouses working together 238

stealing 138

stress 116

submitting to authority 203

success 202

temptation 148

tithing 156

visual aids 39

workaholism 222

worry 116

written reports 36

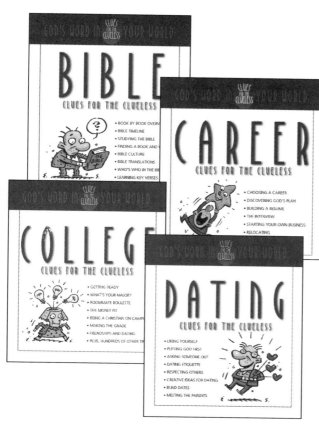